The Sherlock Holmes
Handbook for the Digital Age
*

By John H. Watson & Alan Pearce

9781520140520

Published Alan Pearce November 2016

www.alanpearce.com

D0552825

For
Dee and James Foster
& Kiri

Contents

Prelude

"My dear fellow," said Sherlock Holmes as we sat on either side of the fire in his lodgings at Baker Street. "The Internet should have been the most singular boon to human civilisation since Gutenberg's moveable type printing press but what do we have instead?"

"Lots of amusing cat videos," I answered.

"I shall tell you," said Holmes, ignoring my retort. "Everybody posting the most intimate details of their lives, thoughts and feelings for all and sundry to pour over."

My companion sprang from his cosy chair beside the fire and took down his infernal vaping contraption from the mantelpiece. He adjusted the digital settings and was soon sending thick noxious clouds towards the ceiling. An odour vaguely reminiscent of elderflower filled the room.

"Elderflower," confirmed Holmes. "A blend of my own." He settled back and continued. "Mark my words, Watson, the streets are safer these days because so many common criminals have changed their *modus operandi* and now carry out their despicable crimes online in the comfort of their living rooms."

"But it has also proven to be of considerable benefit to our friends the police," I chimed in.

"Or rather the Internet has become their particular hunting ground. They seek and gather data about every living soul and they make the same elementary mistakes as always." He scoffed scornfully.

"And they simply cannot keep the data safe. Take that Snowden fellow." Holmes pointed his vaping machine in my direction. "No one knows precisely what data he took, and he was just one of thousands of private contractors."

Holmes held up his hand. "Now, I know that you believe that he was acting on the highest principles but can you honestly say the same for every private contractor working for the government?"

I shook my head.

"One can barely read a newspaper these days without some shocking revelation of a new hacking crime, exposing the innocent to the evil designs of criminals."

"But surely," I countered. "The Internet has proven a boon for you in your investigations. Just look at how you can follow people around now – a fellow's precise movements – or how you can take over and control those CCTV security cameras that are ubiquitous these days. I would venture that the Internet has entirely changed your own *modus operandi*."

"Not entirely, my dear Doctor. I still have this." Holmes tapped his temple with the mouthpiece of his vaping machine. "But I would venture, Watson, that the Internet is both a curse for the common man and a blessing for the world of investigation."

"Then why not write it all down?" I ventured. "Why not share your knowledge and know-how with the denizens of cyberspace and let them see how to protect themselves from the criminals and avoid the prying gaze of policemen and spies? They might even learn to become great detectives themselves."

Holmes laughed. "Or perhaps, Watson, you might prefer to write it up yourself, as is your want." He had risen from his chair and was standing between the parted blinds gazing down into the dull neutral-tinted London street.

'Watson," Holmes declared, turning slowly to face me. "It is simplicity itself."

My friend came and stood above me. "After all, it is little more than plain old common sense and a few good programs. I think you can handle that."

'Well," I hesitated. "I was rather thinking that you might apply your prodigious brain to the task."

"And so I shall, Watson. But you will take copious notes and you shall make it available to the *hoi polloi*."

*

So it was that I obtained permission to lay down the most instructive and singular handbook for the Digital Age.

John H. Watson MD
Baker Street
London
November 2016

CHAPTER ONE
My Life is an Open Book

I had only just slipped out of my wet mackintosh and was settling myself comfortably before the fire when Holmes suddenly demanded to see my smartphone.

"Try your inside, left-hand breast pocket," suggested my friend the instant I began patting myself down. I pulled it free and handed it across.

"I see you favour the iPhone. Any particular reason for that?" he asked.

"I rather think them stylish," I ventured. "Aren't they all much of a muchness?"

Holmes chuckled. "It is difficult for a man to have any object in daily use without leaving the impress of his individuality upon it."

"I dare say," said I, unlacing my damp shoes and placing them near to the fire.

Holmes tapped briefly on the screen and then stretched back into his chair, a look of intense scrutiny on his face. He was silent for a long time. Finally he spoke.

"I see you had roast pork for luncheon on Sunday with your delightful new friend. A very handsome woman I must say."

I felt blood rush to my cheeks. "Well," I muttered. "How could you possibly know that?"

He continued. "Tut, tut, Doctor. You have not been to the gym, not once this week. But you have been a moderately frequent visitor to the Fox and Hounds." Holmes stroked the screen and began to smile.

"Your mother's maiden name is Brydon and she was born in London, as were you. Oh, I missed your birthday on the eighth. So sorry about that. I won't embarrass you by mentioning your age."

—

Holmes held up the iPhone for my inspection. "Here is a picture of your somewhat conventional Victorian semi-detached house with your rather garish red motor car parked on the drive." He tapped the screen again and continued.

"And here is a photograph of your practice in Queen Anne Street where you arrive punctually every morning bang on the stroke of nine, except last Thursday when you were nearly thirty minutes late."

"I took my shoes in for repair. My lovely brogues. The heel had come off. But hang on, I didn't take those photographs of my house nor my practice. How did you get them?"

"Google Earth," Holmes explained. "And you had your shoes repaired at that new place near the station. I imagine they will be ready this Wednesday."

"Stop, stop," I declared. "This is positively unsettling. And how did you get into my 'phone in the first place?"

"Elementary, my dear friend. I have seen you pick up and play with your device countless times, and each time when you do you tap the screen in a particular manner. From the movement of your fingers, I surmised that it was either 7-6-5-4 or, as I correctly deduced, 4-3-2-1."

"And what about all the other things? Roast pork, for goodness sake. How?"

"I see you are a player of *Pokemon Go*," said Holmes. "Do you know that it has full access to your movements and to your camera and, if you log in with your Google ID, it can access your contacts as well? And did you know that government agencies and certain criminal elements piggyback on the data in these amusements and use it to track their targets?"

"Well," I muttered. "I haven't played it for weeks."

"But I did not need to access that," said an amused Holmes. "I looked in your Instagram application and saw that you had taken several photographs both prior to and immediately after your Sunday repast."

—

"And the gym and the pub?"

"Ah, yes," said my friend. "You leave your Bluetooth connection on all of the time. You allow yourself to be geotagged. All I needed to do was look in your Google+ account – you were automatically logged in – and follow your movements on Google Maps in perfect detail."

"The shoes?"

"Your Google search queries for a suitable cobbler and Google Maps again."

"My mother's maiden name? My date and place of birth?"

"Facebook."

These shocking revelations had left me feeling both cold and numb. I edged my chair closer to the fire.

"No need to look so surprised," laughed Holmes. "After all, you have chosen to carry around with you the finest surveillance apparatus ever devised. Surely, you know that every single thing you do is open to the closest inspection?"

"But if I have nothing to hide, then surely I have nothing to fear." I nodded my chin decisively.

Holmes pulled himself from the chair and stretched for his own Android 'phone. "Do you have any idea who coined that much-repeated phrase?" he asked.

"Not the foggiest."

"Then I challenge you to a race. Who can find the original of that phrase in the fastest time." He handed me back my iPhone.

Holmes nodded to indicate that the race was suddenly on. I fumbled and finally opened my Safari browser. I noticed Holmes put down his 'phone and settle back contentedly in his chair before I had barely begun.

Moments later I was shocked by what I read. "Oh my goodness," I declared. "I have just quoted Hitler's propaganda chief, Joseph Goebbels. Well I never."

"Close," grinned Holmes. "But no coconut. As it happens, Herr Goebbels was evidently an admirer of that most excellent American novelist Upton Sinclair. Allow me to read to you from his *The Profits of Religion: An Essay in Economic Interpretation*, written in 1918 when young Joseph was a mere student and fawning over a local Jewish girl."

Holmes stretch himself forward and quickly memorised the passage. He then looked me directly in the eyes. *"Not merely was my own mail opened, but the mail of all my relatives and friends – people residing in places as far apart as California and Florida. I recall the bland smile of a government official to whom I complained about this matter: 'If you have nothing to hide you have nothing to fear'."*

My friend was suddenly on his feet and looming above me. "What do you say to that, Doctor? Nothing new under the sun, eh? The powers-that-be have been spying upon the populace since the dawn of time. Only now you are making it child's play for them," Holmes sneered.

I ran my tongue across my pallet. My mouth was bone dry. "All right," I chimed in. "I take your point." I flopped back in my chair and looked up at Holmes.

"But anyway it's swings and roundabouts," I expounded. "I give away a little information that's hardly of any practical value – where I get my shoes repaired, for example – and I get access to the entire Internet, to so much. Our lives have been immeasurably improved. I consider that a fair trade off."

"And the amusing cat videos," quipped Holmes.

"No," I protested. "Access to the greatest source of learning the world has ever known, to new friends and the free flow of thoughts and ideas among peoples. That sort of thing."

Holmes raised an imperious eyebrow towards me. "Tea," he suggested. "That's what you need. Nothing like a nice cup of tea to soften a surprise. I'll call for Mrs Hudson."

CHAPTER TWO
The Three Threats

A measured step was heard upon the stairs and Holmes sprang from his chair.

"Mrs Hudson you are a veritable life-saver. The Doctor here is in urgent need of a cup of hot sweet tea."

"Goodness," exclaimed Mrs Hudson as she bustled through the door and stood holding a heavy tray laden with cosied-teapot, sugar bowl, milk jug and our favourite mugs. I discretely noted the biscuits.

"Has the Doctor had a nasty shock, then? There's nothing better than a nice cup of tea. I've put a few Hobnobs on the plate as well."

Holmes took the tray and placed it on the occasional table before the fire.

"Not as yet, Mrs Hudson. But I fear he shall before the day is out."

Holmes ushered the landlady back through the door. Turning towards the fire he quickly grabbed himself a biscuit and settled back in his chair.

"You are absolutely right, my dear Watson, when you say the Internet is a marvellous thing. All that knowledge, the ability to share thoughts and ideas across the globe regardless of borders or boundaries."

"Well, yes."

"But it has been subverted, Watson. Subverted in the most insidious manner. The glorious ideals of the early days have all but been forgotten. The Internet has become a sinister and dangerous place – a grotesque parody of all that it originally promised."

"Oh, surely you are laying it on a bit thick."

"The Internet – our greatest tool of emancipation – has been transformed into the most menacing facilitator of totalitarianism."

I could only laugh.

"Open your eyes, Watson. We are living in a postmodern surveillance dystopia from which escape for all but the most skilled individuals is impossible."

"And can you escape, Holmes?" I asked, crossing my legs and examining the toe of my old sock. "Or are you trapped like the rest of us, like a fly in amber?"

Holmes did not reply. He rubbed his hands and his eyes glistened.

"There are three main threats, my dear Doctor. Let us examine them one at a time." He leaned forward in his chair with an expression of extraordinary concentration upon his clear-cut, hawk-like features. His eyes bore into mine.

"Threat Number One." Holmes held up an index finger. "I call this the NSA Factor. Cast your mind back to the old East Germany when the Stasi secret police ruled the roost. People couldn't – and didn't – speak openly because they never knew who was listening. Do you imagine, Watson, that this had an effect on the way people behaved? Did people keep their thoughts and feelings to themselves?"

"Yes, I imagine they did."

"And what of North Korea today? Can they speak their minds and not expect a knock at the door?"

"No, I doubt that very much."

"Well, Watson, we have the self-same thing happening today on the Internet. We've all seen the Edward Snowden revelations. We all know we're being monitored all of the time. And this is having a terrible effect on the Internet."

"Well, I don't see any great protests." The tea had brewed long enough so I reached across and lifted the cosy. Holmes sat back while I filled our cups, having first added a dash of milk. I let Holmes help himself to sugar.

"Perhaps," said Holmes. "You would like to take part in a little experiment?"

"Of course. Why not?"

"Next time you send an email – to your Mum, say – include the words *Bomb Kill Prime Minister Thursday* and let's see how long it takes for them to come and get you, shall we?"

"Oh, poppycock," I exclaimed.

"And your Mum, Watson. They will come for her. Let me know how you get on. Did a SWAT team come and kick the door down? Did you find yourself on an airline no-fly list? Have your bank accounts been frozen? Did nothing happen? Or so you think. Keep me posted, do."

"So what are you saying, Holmes, that they read everybody's emails?"

"Yes, just like they read the letters of the friends and family of Upton Sinclair."

"Oh, really."

"Of course they read emails." Holmes hooted and took several seconds to settle himself. "There isn't anything that they can't see, Watson, not on the Surface Web at any rate."

"Surface Web?"

"The Internet that you use. There are others, you know."

"I think you need to slow down a bit." The tea was going down a treat. I took a lengthy sip and savoured the dark tang in my mouth.

Holmes dropped back in his chair and formed a temple with his hands. "All sophisticated security services monitor Internet traffic within their own countries. The US and it's Five Eyes partners monitors *all* communication globally, including the complete contents of private emails, cell phone calls and Internet searches, plus all the personal data trails from parking receipts, bank transfers, travel itineraries and bookstore purchases."

"Who on earth are the Five Eyes?" I desired to know.

"Including the United States, they are Britain, Canada, Australia and New Zealand. They tap directly into the undersea cables and into the satellite links. Into every conceivable means of communication."

I gave Holmes one of my quizzical looks.

"And if they ever need to join the dots, it helps to have all the dots from the past to draw upon. After all, data storage is remarkably inexpensive these days. This means that they can go back in time and listen in on 'phone calls or read messages that were made or sent long before the target was ever under suspicion."

"The correct medical term is 'paranoia', Holmes." Now I laughed. "These are all countries that abide by the rule of law."

"In one sense you are right, Watson," smiled Holmes. "Legally, just the bare bones of the communications are monitored – the who sent what and when, the so-called meta-data. But, although they may not be open about this, all agencies are now looking directly into the message itself, looking for the expected and the unexpected in all our online communications and activities. If they did not make use of this singular opportunity they would not be very good at their jobs."

I tentatively dunked a Hobnob into the strong tea and nodded confirmation.

"They collect information on every citizen and mine it for a variety of indicators, ostensibly terrorism, but the tax authorities, local councils and every other State Tom, Dick and Harry – not to mention the contractors and corporations – can access this data and then build profiles on you."

"I don't think that you should make light of the threat of terrorism, Holmes. You only have to look at the news to see what's happening. It's the modern scourge."

"My dear fellow, I say that if they are monitoring every one of us then they are missing the point."

"Which is?"

"They are looking in the wrong place, Watson. There is absolutely no point in reading your dear mother's emails or monitoring her on Facebook because – patently – she isn't up to no good. The terrorists and the criminals, on the other hand, do not communicate this way. No terrorist worth his salt is going to give anything away in an email or on the telephone. The thought is preposterous. "

"So what do they do then, Holmes?" I had left the biscuit to soak too long and now, to my disappointment, it had broken away like a crumbling iceberg, tumbling to the bottom of the mug. "Do they use these other Internets that you speak of? Do they have some special tools or techniques? Pray tell."

"I fear, Watson, that we are getting ahead of ourselves. All in good time." Now Holmes held up two fingers. "Threat Number Two. Rampant Commercialisation."

"Big Business?" I put in. "Another one of your pet hates. I think that it is fair to point out that Big Business – no matter how you care to paint them – not only contribute a veritable fortune to the coffers in taxes but they drive innovation. The world could simply not exist without them."

"You will have noticed, my friend, how governments are only too happy to protect these supposed contributors to the coffers, the record companies and the film industry being two examples."

Holmes became animated, using his hands to chastise an imaginary fat cat. "But rather than adapt to the changes in technology and move with the times, these captains of industry vigorously cling to their old and dying business models and the State is happy to oblige in tracking down and persecuting those who have actually bothered to move with the times."

Holmes turned and indicated the elegant illuminated world globe that cast a comforting trail of light across the bearskin rug.

"Imagine if the State had made the same moves to protect the steam boiler makers or the whale oil trade," he smiled. "We would not have electricity today. So much then for innovation."

Holmes stretched for another biscuit. "And has something else not escaped your attention? Surely you recall all the hoo-ha surrounding corporations like Google and Amazon and a veritable host of others for not paying their taxes?"

I did have to laugh at that. I began fishing for the lost half Hobnob with my teaspoon and nodded for Holmes to press on.

"Once upon a time," he said. "There were hundreds of small oil companies, all drilling for oil. These days the oil business is in the hands of a few giant corporations. The Big Boys took over. And this is what is happening to the Internet."

Holmes paused to savour his dry Hobnob. "Instead of an information super-highway, we're looking at an expensive toll road. We're heading for the Pay TV model – one nice fast flashy Internet for those that can afford it and a rather rubbishy slow one for those that can't."

"Even so," said I. "People can chose to pay for things if they wish. Take YouTube for instance. I don't pay a penny for that and I can watch all manner of entertainments including some jolly good television dramas from the old days."

"Watson, Watson," said Holmes acting exasperated the way he might with a recalcitrant child. "Every time you visit a page on the Internet – be it YouTube or *The New York Times* – they quietly plant a Cookie in your device. This Cookie, despite its' rather homely name, will follow you everywhere you go. It will note which other sites you visit, which forums and chat rooms, what you like to buy and what you chose to read. This is all vital information, Watson."

Holmes pointed to my steaming shoes beside the fire. "It wants to know which shoes you buy and where you shop – and even where you get your shoes repaired – because this all forms a bigger picture in the giant data-bases that link your voting history to your income, education and shopping preferences. This digital life of yours is then sold off so you can be micro-targeted with tailor-made advertisements."

Holmes got up from his chair and began to pace the room. He swivelled on his heels and pointed what appeared to be a reproachful finger in my direction. "It is true, Watson, when they say *If you are not paying then you are the product.*"

"I still don't feel that troubled." I slurped down the last of the tea, swirling the Hobnob mush amid the dregs.

"Your email account is with Gmail, I believe. With Google?"

"Yes it is and I am very happy with it thank you very much."

"Do you mind that they read your emails and sell on what they learn to others?"

"I don't think that they do."

"You have been listening I trust?" inquired Holmes. "Let me give you an example of getting something for free. You email a friend and mention Venice. Next thing you know you're being bombarded with advertisements for cheap flights and hotels in Venice. They pop up on news websites, on YouTube and every conceivable place."

"I could see that might be advantageous."

"Or you look up the symptoms of haemorrhoids but then for the rest of your life they never let you forget. At any time somebody might be looking over your shoulder and up pops some promotional material to ease your embarrassing affliction."

"I could always unsubscribe to their emails."

"Yes, and suddenly they know that you really exist, rather than just an entry in a long list of email addresses that they have acquired. You have popped your head above the parapet. Now they can seriously target you; they can begin spear phishing."

"Like Eskimos?" I chanced.

"Picking you out of the herd and going for your vitals," exclaimed Holmes.

"So what?" I asked. "You expect me to believe that I am living under some all-seeing microscope and that I am being kept and tended like a milch cow; that I am being harvested for cash?"

"Precisely, Watson. There you have it."

I bent to examine the teapot. There was just enough for the two of us. I poured a generous splash of milk and then topped up our mugs. Holmes now held up three fingers. "Threat Number Three."

He side-stepped across the room and pulled his Stradivarius and bow from their battered case. Holmes examined the strings for a moment and then a long, deeply discordant and melancholic wail set my teeth on edge.

"Criminals and the Disturbed," announced Holmes.

He put the violin and its bow back in their case and came to join me again beside the fire. "This is my smartphone, Watson," said he holding it up for my inspection. "Do you notice anything out of the ordinary?"

"Aside from it being rather tatty you mean?"

"This piece of black tape that covers the forward facing camera and the one at the rear," pointed Holmes. "Why do you think it is here?"

"Well, I assumed it was broken and that you were too stingy it go and get a new one."

"Not so, my dear Watson. Everything has a purpose. Would you care to guess at the purpose here?"

"No, I give up. Please tell me."

"It is to stop people looking upon me and from preventing them following my doings."

"And do you hear voices as well, Holmes?" I chuckled. "How are these imaginary people looking at you?"

Holmes gave a boisterous laugh. "No, my dear doctor I am not paranoid. This threat is as real as any in the dastardly escapades that have faced us in our long association." He indicated the iPhone resting in my lap.

"Be so good as to open your preferred search engine."

"Is Google acceptable?"

"Yes, for the moment it is. Go to Google Images and type this precisely: *zuckerberg + laptop + tape*. What do you see?" my friend asked.

"Well, I see a rather nerdy-looking chap holding up what appears to be a window frame or some similar contraption."

Holmes snatched the iPhone from my grasp and – tapping the screen and spreading open his fingers like a magician revealing a bunch of paper flowers or soaring white dove – he expanded the photograph.

"What do you make of that, Doctor? Mr Zuckerberg by-the-by happens to be the controlling giant behind Facebook and so much else. I imagine that with his startling wealth he can command and employ the brightest brains in the world of technology. And yet what have we here?"

Holmes thrust the screen under my nose.

"It is tape," he declared. "And please note that it is 'low-tech' because this is something that you can actually rely upon."

Holmes dropped back in his chair, a satisfied calmness to his bird-like features. "Mr Zuckerberg – the sixth wealthiest man on Planet Earth – is blocking his forward facing camera with sticky tape because he does not want people looking at him. Do you suppose, Doctor, that he too is paranoid?"

"Quite possibly," I mused. "Although I would need to examine him in some detail."

"Now the big question, of course, is why are any of us doing this? And just who are these people attempting to look in on our lives?"

"I am all ears," I told him.

"Do you ever get those 'phone calls supposedly from the Windows Company telling you that somehow your computer is interfering with the Internet and needs adjustment and usually an Indian or other Sub-Continent accent is discernable?"

"Why, yes. I get them all the time."

"Can you imagine what their game is Watson?"

"Beats me."

"They are playing upon your gullibility. In the first place there is no Windows Company. Windows is a registered trademark of the Microsoft Corporation so already – from the word go – a person should be alert and on guard."

"But what is their aim?"

"They lead you along and have you either do their dirty work for them, Watson, by opening your computer to *Remote Access* via the *Settings* or they will have you visit a phoney Internet page whereby you will download a rather nasty piece of work known as a *Remote Access Trojan*, or in popular parlance a RAT."

"A rat, Holmes? My word."

"From that moment onwards they have complete control over your computer, be it a conventional desktop or something more compact."

"I always put the 'phone straight down," I told him.

My friend gave a sardonic chuckle. "It depends upon my mood, Watson. If my day is proving to be interminably dull I like to have a little fun with them."

"What sort of thing, Holmes?"

"Sometimes I employ my little girls' voice…"

"Oh, your little girls' voice is utterly convincing. Uncanny."

"I like to say things like *My Mummy won't wake up. She's on the kitchen floor. Mummy won't wake up.* And then I cry a little."

"Well, I don't think that's very nice at all," I swiftly warned him. "Poor chap on the receiving end will probably have nightmares 'till the end of his days. You might induce a stroke."

"Then he should not have tried to scam me, Watson. He can have a taste of his own medicine for attempting to spy upon me and suck my bank accounts dry."

"I do admit, Holmes, that I find this disturbing."

"You have heard nothing yet, dear Doctor." He handed me back my iPhone. "Go now to Google Videos and type in the following: *computer + rat + trolling.* Now what do you see?"

"Gracious me," I exclaimed. "First off here is a tutorial of some kind showing how to plant a RAT in a victim's computer."

"And what else?" asked Holmes.

"Well, I am shocked I must say. Do they allow this sort of thing to stay up on the Internet?"

Holmes sprang forward and came to look over my shoulder. "These poor, sad victims that you see here are known as 'RAT Slaves' and some of the more disturbed and depraved elements in society prey upon them, twisting their minds and in extreme cases driving these tortured souls to an early grave." Holmes nodded decisively.

"By what means?" I needed to know, feeling a chill run down my spine.

"Having taken control of their device, these demented fiends scare the living daylights out of their victims by making chilling ghost-like or wailing baby noises in the middle of the night."

"Surely not."

"They hijack the victim's online persona and send out hate-mail insulting their best friends and employers. They post the most palpable nonsense all over social media, turning friends and family against them. The ultimate aim is to drive these poor miserable individuals beyond the point of despair. And they are only limited by their sick imaginations. What else do you observe, Doctor?"

I quickly turned my iPhone off and rested it beside the tea tray on the occasional table before the fire. "I simply do not wish to look at people being tormented. There are young females there, screaming their heads off. Shocking I must say."

"Come, come, Doctor. I know you have a stronger stomach than that." Holmes looked forlornly at the cold tea pot and settled back with resignation into his chair.

"Today's sex stalkers and the like," he announced. "They do not have to hide in the shrubs anymore, not when they can sip a *latte* at Starbucks and stalk multiple victims in real time on the free Wi-Fi."

Holmes could not settle in his chair. He lifted himself repeatedly from the seat in a futile attempt at comfort. Finally, he was up again and doing a little stalking around himself, to and fro across the comfy sitting room.

"All manner of sick and demented people now have access to the most powerful and sophisticated tools. What was once the preserve of law enforcement and the intelligence agencies is now readily available to anybody who can handle a digital crypto currency."

"How so?" I demanded. "A fellow can't just pop down the shops and buy half-a-pound of RATS."

"In the realms of cyber space, I think he can." Holmes clasped his hands behind his back, pulling his ornate scarlet dressing gown tight to his chest.

"Any unseasoned stalker only has to enquire within the right forums and chat rooms and in no time he – or perhaps she – would find themselves on a very dark and dangerous path, down into the nether realms of the Internet. RATS are two a penny here and small fry at that."

"I am intrigued, Holmes. Are you referring to the Dark Web?"

"You are nothing but perceptive, Doctor. But that perilous journey must await another day." Holmes looked at the screen of his bandaged Android. "I am due to dine with Mycroft *ce soir* and must make haste. If you will excuse me."

CHAPTER THREE
The Lock Down

Holmes had sent me a rather cryptic message regarding a rendezvous on a particular bench facing the Round Pond in Kensington Gardens at two-twenty sharp on a broody and deathly calm Wednesday. I looked again at my watch. I had two full minutes to spare and occupied myself in admiring the few small sailboats that drifted leisurely across the cold, grey water.

Beside me on the bench a disreputable old tramp set to whistling Mozart's *Eine Kleine Nachtmusik*. I then made the cardinal error of catching his eye. He abruptly cut short the ascending Mannheim 'rocket' theme and edged up beside me. I was immediately aware of that particular dank, musty odour reminiscent of hot, exhausted solders that had been so familiar to me in Afghanistan.

"Got any spare change?" The tramp demanded gruffly.

And then the penny dropped. "Holmes, you have made a fool of me yet again. You have done me up like a kipper." We both chuckled. "Well I must say that is a capital disguise but what, pray, are you doing in that particular get-up?"

"I am on assignment, my dear friend. No peace for the wicked," winked Holmes. "I am engaged upon a rather convoluted case involving a dowager and a considerable sum of money needing to be returned to its' rightful owner. We have time yet."

I settled back on the bench and watched a delightful sloop-rigged miniature yacht tack abruptly to starboard.

"Did you bring your iPhone?" asked my friend.

I tapped my inside, left-hand breast pocket. Holmes nodded and I slipped it out for his scrutiny.

"Now, correct me if I am mistaken but your primary consideration in the selection of a suitable smartphone is 'style', yes?"

"Well, not entirely Holmes. There are other considerations. It's supposed to tie up with my iPad although I confess I can never make it happen. Something always eludes me." And then a thought did occur to me. "I believe that they are less susceptible to the common viruses."

"So right you are, Watson. There are more viruses designed specifically for Androids because there are more Android devices in circulation. That said, we are all equally at risk."

"So why don't you have one, Holmes?"

"Because I do not entirely trust the Apple Corporation, nor any product made under conditions so harsh that anti-suicide nets are called upon to prevent the workers doing harm to themselves. For another thing, you cannot remove the memory card from the iPhone but can from an Android."

"And why should anybody wish to do that, Holmes?"

"Simply because if your 'phone fell into the wrong hands they would find it so much easier to see who your contacts are, to read your diary and make note of your appointments. With an Android, you might have two sim cards – an important one with all your contacts and a not-so-important one that would not give anything away. You could swap them around as you saw fit."

"I suppose."

"And you cannot remove the battery on the iPhone." Holmes held up a grimy hand. "And why would you want to do that, you might ask?"

I wasn't sure.

"Because, even if you believe you have switched off your 'phone and that it is dead to the world, quietly in the background a nasty little program may be lurking, transmitting your whereabouts and ear-wigging on your conversations. That is why, Watson."

"And you have the gall to accuse me of inflicting my lurid tales upon a long-suffering public," I huffed.

"Soon," said Holmes. "We will examine this area in more detail and you will see for yourself. But, for now, my intention is to fine-tune your iPhone. And, for the benefit of your readers, everything that I am about to disclose is equally valid for the Android user."

"Right you are."

"We are going to Clear Out, Load Up, Lock Down and Run Silent," announced my friend. "I noticed the other day that you have many unnecessary applications, starting with *Pokemon Go* which you claim not to have played in over a week. Get rid of it. And clear out all those unused applications, especially the games."

Holmes peered over me while I began to delete them one by one.

"Watson, you must be very careful of what you install. Most are free or temptingly inexpensive because the developers make their money by letting in third parties – the advertisers, the criminals, all sorts. And these are the very applications, or 'apps' as they are known, which carry out secret tasks and join with other apps to paint a fuller picture of your life."

I hesitated, my finger poised to remove the very amusing game that involves throwing chickens through hoops and all sorts of other high jinks but Holmes was too fast for me.

"Take *Angry Birds* for example and I see you have that. There was a phoney version doing the rounds, ringing up premium rate 'phone numbers on the sly. It cost some people a tidy fortune."

"Well, I'll get rid of that Holmes. How can a chap tell if this sort of thing is happening?"

"You might pay attention to how swiftly the battery is depleting and also one clue is an extra warmth about the device which means it is working hard on some secret task. Just get rid of the rotten things and don't put them back."

"Right you are."

"Now you need to Load Up," announced Holmes. "You need to install the right software. Take anti-spyware and anti-virus programs, for instance. Have you ever taken the time to install any extra precautions?"

"Can't say that I have."

The famous Holmes index finger wagged before my eyes. "There is absolutely no excuse not to. They will alert you the very instant somebody with ill intentions sends you an infected email, and they will apply the brakes should you suddenly find yourself heading off to an unbidden Internet page where you may become the unwitting victim of a malicious download."

Endless questions flashed as one to my mind.

"You don't have to cough up for the Premium editions," Holmes declared. "I tend to apply the benefit of the doubt in this instance, Watson, and I accept the free versions especially when they come 'open-source', meaning some clever IT fellows – some chaps whose brains work differently from mine – can have a jolly good fish around inside and seek out hidden 'backdoors' and the like."

"I see."

"So, to that end, install the free version of Avast. That's the one I currently favour and be sure to install it on all of your digital devices."

Holmes had me seek out the program via Google and install it there and then. But I had a burning question. "Why are we doing all this outside in the cold by this dreary pond when we might be snug as a bugs at Baker Street?" I pulled the collar of my Dunn & Co overcoat tight about me.

"Because, my dear fellow, we are marginally safer when we use the 4G signal than if we were using Wi-Fi, especially so as you have not as yet installed the next vital step."

"Which is?"

"An elementary VPN, a Virtual Private Network, Watson. I favour the free version of Hotspot Shield. This will effectively send you down a small rabbit hole. You connect directly to these peoples' server the very instant you attempt to go online. From that moment forth all your activities are hidden by means of powerful encryption from any snoop or skilled onlooker."

I looked it up without delay and began to install the 'app'.

"It also has the added advantage," confided Holmes. "Of allowing you to view banned content such as Internet sites the government doesn't want you to see and you can access Twitter and Facebook mobile if their services are ever blocked locally."

"How so?"

"Because once you are down the rabbit hole you are no longer here in a chill and overcast London. You might be anywhere on the planet that Hotspot Shield sends you."

"Got that now, Holmes," I smiled. I was finding it all rather too easy. "What next?"

"Back to your search engine, Watson. Now type *"open whisper systems"* + *signal*, got it?"

I travelled from page to page and was finally able to declare, "I am downloading it from the Apple Store now. Another free product, Holmes?"

"Only in that you do not need to pay to download it. This one is crowd-funded and, as the name implies, it is open-source. Trust me on this one."

"Righto," I declared. "What's it for?"

Holmes took the iPhone from me and swiftly his fingers set about an adjustment of the *Settings*. Then he tapped his nose knowingly. "This shall be our Hot Line. We will scramble our calls. Expect to hear from me."

"Gosh. Anything else?" I asked. "I confess that it is getting a tad chilly."

"Lock Down," said Holmes. "This is where it gets a little technical but nothing that you cannot handle, I promise."

"You will be pleased to learn, Holmes," said I as a thought momentarily flashed into my mind. "That I have changed the passcode after your little demonstration the other day. Although I had toyed with the idea of making use of the fingerprint security option. You can even draw a picture, I understand, as a means of unlocking the device."

"Yes I am aware of that, Watson." My friend took on his superior air. "And what would you draw, a simple yacht – perchance?"

"Well, yes," I chuckled. "Sitting here, looking at these boats, I must admit that it had crossed my mind what with it being simple to draw and all that."

Holmes guffawed loudly and quickly checked himself, lowering his voice. "Better that than the first of the two most popular motifs – which is the human penis, Watson."

"Blow me," I declared. "What is the world coming to?"

"But – you being a medical man – would probably make a dog's dinner of it by going into such detail as to highlight the *corpora cavernosa*."

"Perhaps then I should select the fingerprint option," I opined.

"*Au contraire, mon ami*. With a copy of a fellow's fingerprints and access to a 3-D printer it is fully possible to reproduce a facsimile that could easily fool the iPhone and most any similar devices, including anything you might see in the subterraneous recesses of 85 Albert Embankment, Vauxhall."

With subtle ease Holmes swiftly assumed a nonchalant air. I followed his gaze to see a rather large party of Oriental schoolgirls heading around the delightful curve of the pond and in our direction, and looking as if to dawdle.

My friend then resumed his whistling but with such a painful resonating pitch that I felt the hairs stand erect on the back of my neck. I discretely watched as Holmes directed his world-renowned withering glare towards the party which may have been either Japanese or Chinese for it is sometimes difficult to tell.

"Well, that worked Holmes," I declared in admiration when they hurriedly set upon their way.

"Quickly, Watson. For the clock runs against us. Open your *Settings*." He indicated the forgotten iPhone that lay in my chilled and stiff hands.

"Go to *Wi-Fi* and untick *Ask to join Networks*. Now turn off *Geotagging* and *GPS location*. Then go to *Privacy*, *Location* and untick *Use my Location*. You don't need them unless you are looking for the nearest Nepalese restaurant or whatnot."

Holmes looked about him and brought his swarthy and repellent face close to mine. "Never, Watson, never allow any of your devices to connect with the office network or with any other computer."

I nodded to show that he had my tacit agreement.

"And, above all else, never – repeat – never avail yourself of free chargers, no matter where you find them, airports, hotels, bars, wherever."

Holmes stood in preparation for his departure. He bent and gathered the soiled and dog-eared bags that lay strewn all around us.

"And, Watson, remember, on no account are you to let that iPhone out of your sight. Not for a second. Not while you slip to the loo or pop upstairs for a clean handkerchief."

"But Holmes," I called. "What about Running Silent? What of that?"

"That, my friend, shall have to wait upon another time and place."

With that, Sherlock Holmes turned in the direction of the Oriental schoolgirls and was soon out of sight.

CHAPTER FOUR
Running Silent

I was in the act of returning my library books and debating whether to amuse myself with the monthly periodicals when I was startled by an insistent buzzing in my inside, left-hand breast pocket.

"Hello, Holmes," I enounced. "I am getting the hang of this 'phone-scrambling malarkey now, this code-word lock thing. Over."

"My dear Watson, you do not have to keep saying 'Over' each time you complete a sentence."

"Sorry, Over. Oh, sorry."

"Look here, Watson, can you meet me outside the British Museum in, say, half-an-hour?"

"Well, as luck would have it, I am in Town. What's afoot?" I enquired.

"I shall explain everything when you get here."

"How shall I recognise you, Holmes? Over."

"My dear fellow, today I shall appear as Sherlock Holmes. And, besides, I shall find you."

"Right you are, Holmes. I shall set off now."

"Don't spare the horses, Watson. This one is imperative."

"What's so imperative about a special exhibition of Early Etruscan Metalwork?" I wanted to know.

"These, my dear Doctor," said Holmes, displaying two free tickets. "Expire this very day and we would be foolish not to avail ourselves of a little culture. After all, the Etruscans were the masters of bronze. I believe we shall see a rare example of a miniature canopic urn."

"I am all a-tingle."

—

While I kept my iPhone safely tucked inside my left-hand breast pocket, Holmes had his tatty-looking Android out in the open. We handed over our tickets and sauntered into the display. Holmes made a bee-line for a cabinet at the far end of the room.

"Here you go, Watson," he marvelled. "What are they depicting on this funeral urn, eh?"

"Can't quite make it out, really." I shrugged.

"A Dionysian Revel, Watson." Holmes appeared mildly disappointed at my lack of knowledge in this particular field.

"They are off their rockers," he laughed. "The Etruscans used intoxicants and other trance-inducing techniques to remove inhibitions and social constraints, liberating the individual to return to a natural state. The Dionysian Revel?"

"Fascinating, I must say."

Holmes consulted the guidebook and soon we were making haste for a distant display.

"Watson, do you remember that Cartwright fellow? The chap with an amazing abundance of white hair?"

"Well, yes, but I'd be a bit vague on the details. What about him?"

Holmes had his Android open in front of him. "I recall that his first name was Dominic but what was his middle name?"

"How in heaven do you expect me to remember a detail like that?" I asked.

"I shall look him up in my *Contacts*." Holmes gave me the decisive nod.

It was just then that a security guard or some other kind of officious fellow came up to us. "Excuse me but you can't take photos in 'ere. Sign says clearly, No Photos."

Holmes scoffed. "But, my good man, who is taking photographs? Are you suggesting that I am doing so?"

"You got your 'phone out. You can't take photos. Put it away or I'll have to ask you to leave."

"Look, my man," said Holmes. "I am examining my *Contact*s. We are in the midst of a debate about the middle name of an acquaintance of ours. Do you see a photography application active and in operation?"

"Please, sir. Just put it away or I'll have to ask you to leave."

Holmes thrust his Android into the man's surprisingly small hands which is often a sign of *acrodysostosis*.

"Look here, please avail yourself," said Holmes. "Tell me, can you see any prohibited applications running? No," he declared without giving the man a chance. "I think not."

He turned suddenly to me while snatching back his Android. "Watson, it is time that we leave."

With that, Holmes took my arm and ushered me back out into the sullen drizzle of a Bloomsbury afternoon.

"Plonk yourself down here," said Holmes indicating a bench away from the window. "What can I get you?"

"I'm really not sure, Holmes. I can't see a menu on the table. What sort of things do they have?"

"Burgers and nuggets." Holmes appeared impatient. "Ham-burgers, chips, over-sweet deserts and appalling coffee."

"I thought we might go to that nice chop house at Butler's Wharf. Where on earth are we?"

"My dear Doctor, we are in an American fast food franchise. We are in McDonalds."

"Again Holmes, I must ask why?"

"Because of the free Wi-Fi, Watson. That is why. Look, settle yourself down and login. You do not need a passcode. See if the weather is due to pick up any time soon."

"Ask if they have tea, Holmes."

Some little time later my friend returned clutching a brown plastic tray.

"*Voilà*," he declared. "Here you go, Watson. Your first-ever Happy Meal."

"Are you not having anything?" I asked.

Holmes made a disparaging puff. "I wouldn't eat here, my friend. Not for all the tea in China. I only ever pop in to use the loo."

I looked at the curious package and containers atop a sheet of advertising material that covered the tray. "Aren't I missing something, Holmes?"

"Such as?"

"Cutlery." I mimicked the use of knife and fork. "Surely, you do not expect me to eat with my hands."

"Look around you, Watson. This is the modern world. This is the done thing nowadays. When in Rome, eh?"

"I despair, Holmes. I really do." I turned up my nose and applied my attention to the iPhone.

"Don't look now, Watson." Holmes drew me closer. "But there is a young woman wearing a fawn-coloured windcheater just behind you. She is peering into a laptop and lingering over-long with her Sprite Zero. Now, she is either working on her *curriculum vitae* or she is operating a Wi-Fi Sniffer."

"Wi-Fi Sniffer?"

"Precisely."

I creased my brow, indicating that Holmes should elaborate. My friend pulled out his Android, his fingers flashing like lightning.

"I suspect a Pineapple, Watson." A troubled expression came over my friend's face but then he smiled and applied a look of understanding and patience.

"A simple and deviously portable device that can be carried into any hotspot of the kind you find in hotel lobbies, bars, fast food outlets, *etcetera*."

I sat back in wonder.

"The aim of the Pineapple, Watson, is to hoodwink any device such as your iPhone into thinking that it is connecting to a legitimate Wi-Fi access point rather than one-hundred dollars' worth of clever spyware. I also suspect an Evil Twin attack."

"Good heavens, Holmes, and here in a McDonalds." Once more I was taken aback. "And pray tell, what is an Evil Twin attack?"

"You will recall that we have already covered 'Phishing' although I admit not in any great detail."

I concurred.

Holmes peered deep into my eyes, rather like a stage hypnotist. "The Evil Twin," he explained, "is the wireless version of the old phishing scam. It wants you to lock on to its' signal so the operator can intercept all your data as it passes through their network. They want your bank details, Watson. Your credit card details primarily and of course PayPal."

"But am I safe, Holmes? You just had me connect to the Wi-Fi signal here. Surely, I'm at risk."

"Calm yourself, Doctor. You are perfectly safe. Remember that we installed Hotspot Shield?"

"So, I am down the rabbit hole," I marvelled. "She can't see me then, Holmes?"

"You are invisible to her, Watson."

"Well, that's a blessed relief, I can tell you. You had me going for a minute there, Holmes. But that is not why we are here, is it?" I asked my friend.

"Perceptive as always, Doctor." Holmes held up his Android and flicked the screen. "Take a look at these. They are rather good, if I say so myself."

I looked at the screen perplexed. "Holmes," I declared. "Surely you were not taking photographs inside the exhibition?"

My friend snickered. "Yes, and much else besides. But these are for educational purposes only." Holmes continued to flick at the screen. "They have come out rather well, have they not?"

"Well, they look very professional, I must say. Very nicely framed and the lighting is very good. But you have taken dozens of photographs and I didn't see you compose a single image, not once."

"That, my friend, is because I was using a secret camera application. A very sneaky device to be sure. There are numerous versions available for both the Android and iPhone. In this instance, my screen appears to be black. I just tap the screen whenever I want to take a photograph and no one need know a thing."

"Good gosh, Holmes. And none of that camera shutter sound?"

He shook his head. "This particular app, Watson, will also record video in the same manner. You will recall that dullard earlier did not have a clue, not even when he had my device in his hands. Look here."

I looked at the screen.

"Observe, Watson. He is looking directly into the camera. And listen." Holmes adjusted the volume.

"Just put it away or I'll have to ask you to leave."

We both had a good chortle at that. "But tell me, Holmes, what else were you up to?"

Holmes flicked the screen once more. "Even if you had been paying the keenest attention to me, Watson, you would not have seen me activate the secret audio recorder."

I shook my head.

"In this particular instance, I set it with my map application before I left Baker Street and the very instant we stepped over the threshold of the museum my device automatically began recording."

"Well, I must say, this is all very cloak-and-dagger, Holmes. Next thing you will be telling me that you can see in the dark."

"But of course. Here is my night vision app." Holmes then peeled back the sticky tape from the back of his Android. "See here, Watson. Notice that I have affixed a small ring around the camera lens."

Holmes fished around in his pocket and placed three small round items on the Formica table-top. "These are additional lenses. In order to see well at night you need a good lens. They just clip on. I have here a fisheye for a wider field of vision, a powerful zoom and a macro lens which transforms my Android into a highly efficient magnifying glass."

"Well, I am flabbergasted, Holmes. I had no idea these things were available."

"And look at this, Watson. This is *Ear Spy*. I might be sitting here, minding my own business, listening to music with my earphones plugged in and my feet all a-tap but in reality I am amplifying the sound around me and can easily listen in on other people's conversations."

"Astonishing." I snapped back my jaw. "What else have you there?"

"I have all the essentials, everything to turn my seemingly ordinary Android into a high-tech spy tool and counter-surveillance device."

"My head is spinning," I told him.

Holmes lowered his voice. "Right now, Watson, I am waiting for a small steam drifter to reach the South Coast. She slipped into the Bay of Biscay late last night under the cover of dark."

Holmes held his Android closer so that I could see. "With *Ship Finder* I can monitor the position of all manner of vessels from passenger and cargo ships to yachts and gin-palaces."

"Holmes," I said. "I know this is unlikely, but just suppose your 'phone were ever to fall into the wrong hands, they would see all this clever spy equipment and the game would be up."

"Except, my dear friend, all these clever little apps are hidden within a secret compartment deep inside my device."

Holmes noted my confusion. "Obviously, there is no button here saying 'Secret Compartment'. In order to open my safe, all I need do is make a call to a specific number and *hey presto* the hidden vault reveals itself. And should the worst ever come to the worst, there is a self-destruct feature that let's me send a special code to my 'phone and all the data within simply disappears."

"But what if you needed that information, Holmes. Would it be lost forever?"

"No, my dear Watson. Because I have safely backed up my Android to a secure cloud location."

"Like DropBox or the iCloud?" I ventured.

"Not on your life, Watson. They are not to be trusted. There are plenty of other options from Tresorit through to Seafile. These, my friend, can be relied upon."

"And do you not still need passwords, Holmes, to keep everything secure, or is that *passé* now?"

"Of course you do," laughed Holmes. "It is more vital now than ever." He stood suddenly, preparing to depart. "But let us adjourn to more commodious surroundings and I shall show you how to devise a password so fiendishly secure that not even the might of the NSA and all its computing power will be able crack it."

Holmes gave me a sly wink. "That said, Watson, one should never say never."

"I'll attract the waitresses' attention," I told him while looking keenly about me.

"Do not trouble yourself, Watson. That has all been taken care of. You remember that case of the Dowager and the missing fortune that I was telling you about?" said Holmes as he ushered me through the double glass doors and out into the gloom-laden street.

I popped open my umbrella and raised it high so Holmes could come in out of the rain. "Well, that one paid off handsomely, my friend. I am in funds. Your shout next time, Doctor."

CHAPTER FIVE
Pride is the Password

By the time we returned to the comfort of Baker Street the wind and rain were kicking up a storm, rattling the windows and obscuring the street lights in clouds of swirling yellow vapour.

Holmes busied himself with the fire while I perused the nearest bookshelf and sipped at my rum-laced hot chocolate. I selected a first-edition of Jane Austen's *Pride and Prejudice* and came and settled myself beside the now roaring fire.

Holmes soon after came to join me, placing on his lap the jewelled snuff box that had been given to him so long ago by the King of Bohemia and opening the lid. I declined the heady concoctions that he proffered.

"The key to good cyber-security, my dear Doctor, is a secure password that cannot be guessed at or cracked." Holmes drew his clenched forefinger and thumb to an expectant nostril and inhaled deeply.

"A good password should be at least 12 characters long and should contain a mixture of upper and lower case, numerals and symbols."

"Not pets' names or the birthdays of nephews?" I asked provocatively.

"Play Devil's advocate if you must, my friend, but this is deadly serious." Holmes paused to charge the other nostril. "No – on no account – use the names of pets or memorable dates – the very thing that a villain can find on your Facebook page."

I could see that Holmes was secretly struggling to withhold a sneeze. He ploughed on staunchly. "And never use any word that you can find in a dictionary. On no account write down your passwords and do not store them in a dedicated password safe as the very existence of such a thing can draw attention in itself."

"You are not leaving me many options, Holmes," I told him.

Holmes thumbed his nose and placed the jewelled snuff box on the occasional table beside the fire. He looked deep into space for a moment, a penetrating intensity upon his sharp features.

"Make a note of this, Watson. Write down these letters – i-i-a-t-u-a-t-a-s-m-i-p-o-a-g-f-m-b-i-w-o-a-w. Got that?"

"Upper or lower case, Holmes?"

"Lower case. Now do you think you could memorise that?"

I scoffed. "Hardly, Holmes. Although I suppose that if I broke it down into sections and then memorised them one at a time, then I just might."

Holmes stood up and chuckled as he began to pace the room.

"My dear fellow, anybody of reasonable intelligence can easily remember these characters. That book in your lap, Doctor. Please be so good as to open it at the beginning."

I crossed my legs and sat back with the book open in my hands. My eyes fell upon the introductory passage.

Holmes stood facing the window, his hands firmly clasped behind his back and the rain beating a steady tattoo on the glass. *"It is a truth universally acknowledged,"* he declared, *"that a single man in possession of a good fortune must be in want of a wife."*

"Good heavens, Holmes. Those are the very words here on the page before me. You have a prodigious memory to be sure."

My friend came and settled himself before the fire once more. He leaned forward and rested his angular elbows firmly on his knees.

"We now have the initial elements of a secure password," he told me. "And one that is wickedly simple to remember. After all this is one of the most memorable opening passages in English literature."

"It sums up the plot nicely," I added. "But I still don't get it, Holmes."

My friend laughed fit to bust. "Watson, my dear fellow, one takes the initial letter of each word and forms them together. Show me your screen."

I held up my iPhone.

iiatuatasmipoagfmbiwoaw

"*It is a truth universally acknowledged* and all that. Clear as day."

I was beginning to catch on.

"And there we have our starting point, Doctor. Now we must add to this some upper case, numerals and symbols." Holmes swiftly snatched my 'phone and set about adding the extra elements.

"See here, Watson. Now see what I have done." Holmes handed me back my iPhone. I looked at the screen.

£iiatuata9sMipoagfmbiwoaW(@_@)

"You will see that I have added the British Pound Sterling symbol. I have added this for its rarity value. Not every hacker will think to use that." Holmes scoffed.

"Then I have counted nine characters along and there I have inserted the number 9. I have capitalised the M for man and the W for woman because that, too, is simple to remember. And at the end I have added a particular 'smiley face'. I rather think that it resembles an owl."

"Dashed clever, Holmes, I must say but a bit of a mouthful, what?"

"If you want a password that can withstand even the most determined of 'brute force attacks', 'dictionary attacks' or 'exhaustive key searches', Watson, this is your only course of action."

"I could always choose a shorter opening passage, could I not?"

"Yes, Doctor. But not too short. But it gets even more deviously clever. We have here a means of passing on a password without having to actually spell it out."

"How so?"

"Once the recipient understands the principle, Watson, you just need to mention any book that can be found on Amazon or other online book store that allows you to look inside and read the relevant line, thereby receiving the password."

"Give me a practical example, please."

"Suppose, Doctor, that I were to send you an email and happen to mention that I have just finished reading an entertaining book. You would be in the know, so when I mention *Fear and Loathing in Las Vegas* you then know to go look up the opening line."

"I see."

"And your password will be w-w-s-a-b-o-t-e-o-t-d-w-t-d-b-t-t-h."

"Got it."

"But, Watson, do not use the same password for everything. When it comes to higher levels of security – for your email or PayPal account – you need to devise unique passwords for each."

"My heart sinks, Holmes. Must I remember still more?"

Holmes scoffed. "It is simplicity itself. Think of it this way – for your banking account select a book about banking or bankers. *Bonfire of the Vanities* by Tom Wolfe being a good example and again easy to remember. For your email, think of a poem or some such thing about love letters – *letters* being the key aid to your memory."

"Yes, Holmes, I think I get it now."

"Remember to change your passwords regularly and ensure that your browser does not automatically remember passwords. Look in *Settings* and untick *Remember passwords for sites*."

"Should I be taking notes, Holmes?"

"Yes, Watson, I believe your readers will benefit from it."

I swiftly sorted myself out and then pressed my friend to continue.

"When it comes to filling in those online forms it rarely matters if the answers are truthful or not, so there is little reason to give away valuable information that might be used elsewhere."

"Oh, that is crafty but won't it lead to confusion?"

"Aside from tax returns and passport applications, it does not matter one jot. Apart from that, never – absolutely never – use your actual date of birth. This is one of the first things an investigator like myself looks for when tracking an individual. Equally, never give away your mother's maiden name."

I was suddenly abased.

"When they want to know things like your mother's place of birth, your favourite food, first pet, and all that rot, there is a simple solution which gives absolutely nothing away."

"What's that?"

"Let me give you an example. You are filling in a form to join a club or go on holiday and they start wanting to know these things. When they ask *What is Your Favorite Food*? Write *Hudson*. To *Mother's Maiden Name* write *Hudson. First Pet? Hudson. Where Were You Born? Hudson.*"

I shook my head.

"You can remember *Hudson*, it's a doddle and you give nothing away."

Holmes suddenly dived deep into his trouser pocket. He plucked out his Android and smiled at the screen.

"Watson, my dear chap," he announced. "My ship has come in. I must be gone. We must end the tour here for today and – I am sorry to say – that you shall have to venture out again into this inclement weather."

I gave an involuntary shudder.

CHAPTER SIX
We Shall Not be Taken for Fools

It was some days before I heard from Holmes again. I was in the process of selecting several new pairs of socks at the Marks & Spencer's store near Marble Arch when I was alerted by a brief vibration inside my left hand breast pocket.

This time Holmes had sent me a discrete text message via the Signal application. I had only a few brief seconds to reply before the message would disappear for ever.

"Lunch? Criterion. Now. SH"

"Righto," I responded and was soon on my way. The incessant rain had done nothing to reduce the crowds in Oxford Street and I had the Devil's own job to find a cab. In the end I cut my loses and made my way on foot to our favoured eatery. Suffice to say I was dripping wet by the time I arrived thirty minutes later.

"Watson, my dear chap, you have all the attributes of a drowning rat." Holmes helped me struggle out of my mackintosh and placed the umbrella in the stand. "Come, let me help revive you at the Long Bar."

I was just sipping my second whisky and soda and beginning to feel human again when Holmes dropped the subject of the origin of the tantalus and suddenly asked if the words 'Social Engineering' held any meaning for me.

"If I were to guess," I told him. "I would say it had something to do with designing better shopping malls, or hospitals, schools, that sort of thing."

"Not so. Its' meaning is far more insidious."

"Pray tell."

"Social Engineering is the art of playing upon people's gullibility or their natural desire to please. Recollect the telephone calls from the supposed Windows Company. They wanted you to believe that your computer was in urgent need of correction."

"They were trying to plant a RAT in my device."

"Quite so. Recall also the woman in the fawn windcheater with the Wi-Fi Sniffer."

"You described these as Phishing Scams."

"Precisely. And there are no limits to the forms these can take, Watson. Most professional con-artists – much like their sex stalking counterparts – now work online." Holmes' discerning eyes took in the elegant surroundings. A lyrical expression settled in those eyes as he turned them back to me.

"They tug at the heart strings on dating sites, they offer miraculous bargains, and they can pretend to be you, my friend, in a crisis; imploring the acquaintances in your very own contacts book to send money urgently. Usually a wire transfer via Western Union."

"Good heavens, Holmes. But how?"

My friend clenched the fingers of his hand into a hard, tight ball and rested his decisive chin upon his fist. "Understand it this way, Watson. The computer firewalls and the anti-virus programs that we employ are very good and they get better by the day. They are highly efficient at thwarting a casual chancer or even a determined trickster."

"I should hope so, too."

"But, Watson, we are engaged in an ever changing game of cat and mouse. The criminals, the depraved and even our very own government must find ways around the technological barriers. So what do you imagine they do, Watson?"

Holmes gave me no time to think, let alone provide a satisfactory answer,

"I shall tell you, old chap. They go for the weakest link in the chain."

"The human?" I ventured. "They prey on people's gullibility."

"Precisely. And they do this by Social Engineering."

"And is that how I might cop a RAT?"

"Oh, yes. Take the simplest technique. You receive an email. You have just won the Saskatchewan State Lottery. This would be very lucky indeed, especially so as you did not buy a ticket."

"I've had those. But I wouldn't fall for something so obvious."

"Quite so, Watson. So you receive another email. This time the daughter of the recently-deposed Nigerian foreign minister wants to lodge several million US dollars in your bank account for safe keeping."

"Well, I'm hardly likely to fall for that. I wasn't born yesterday."

"Ah, but Watson many do. They are foolish enough to open the accompanying attachment or perhaps they are invited to follow a link to claim their prize." Holmes slapped his hands together, imitating the jaws of a trap.

"And there the scam-artist has them. If they open the attachment a malicious program is suddenly activated. If they follow that link they may fall victim to the 'Drive-By Download' dodge."

I gulped more whisky.

"These malicious programs are taken on-board much as you might a common Cookie. And there is no telling when or where they may strike. It might be a RAT, of course, or it might be a worm-like entity tasked with seeking out your passwords or bank account details."

"But Holmes you are talking of people with presumably low IQs, people who perhaps earn very little money. What great benefit is there in targeting the lower orders?"

Holmes laughed. "These, Watson, are just simple examples to set the scene. But the salient point here is that from the lowliest scammer to the most sophisticated intelligence agent, they all use largely the same Social Engineering techniques. And it is of these that we must all be aware."

"Never let the old guard down, eh?" I examined my empty glass, rolling its base on the polished counter.

"Let me give you an example, Watson. Take the case of the Bahrain human rights activists. These are smart people – doctors like yourself – lawyers, engineers, teachers. They receive emails purporting to be from the *al Jazeera* news network. The reporter is alerting them to the arrest and grisly torture of one of their colleagues. So, human nature being what it is, they are compelled to open the attachment."

"And they fall in the trap?"

"Yes, they do. And in this instance they fall for one of the wickedest of all spy programs, the notorious FinSpy. And the point here, Watson, is that even the brightest of people can be fooled."

"So what happened to the Bahraini activists?"

"Well, they were done for, Watson. A sophisticated RAT – but one so mighty and all-seeing that it requires an export license to be sold overseas – was planted inside their smartphones and laptops."

I shook my head in despair and edged my glass forward across the bar top.

"From that moment onwards, Watson, they were 'owned' as they call it by Bahrain's National Security Agency. These *ghutra*-wearing secret policemen could see every contact, every email ever sent or received and each movement down to the finest detail; their conversations listened in upon."

"But what might one do in such circumstances? If you ignore the email you might miss something vital."

"One must always be observant, my friend. One must seek out the clues." Holmes caught the barman's eye and indicated our empty glasses.

"In the Bahraini case, my friend, the email address was the first and best clue. I happen to know that *al Jazeera* has its own domain name so it would not be using an email address such as melissa.aljazeera@gmail.com."

"Very perceptive, I'm sure."

"One must always pay special attention to the email addresses. For instance, you receive an email seemingly from PayPal. They are telling you that you must urgently confirm your login details."

I nodded knowingly.

Holmes began to swivel on his stool, casting his gaze around the bar and up to the tops of the marble columns that soared above us. "Firstly you must look at the address it has been sent to. Is this the email address that you use for PayPal? If not, destroy that email immediately."

My friend settled back and leaned against the counter. "Invariably, there is a link within the email that you are invited to follow. Examine this closely, Watson. If it is a variation of paypal.com then it may be genuine. If it is something entirely different, again immediately destroy that email."

I thought for a moment and then put in, "I imagine, Holmes, that my best course of action would be to go directly to the PayPal Internet page, the way I would ordinarily. I could login as usual that way. Would I be safe then, Holmes?"

"Bravo, Watson. This is your only course of action. And, while on the subject of email, inform your readers to go to their email *Settings* and disable *Display Emails in HTML*."

"HTML?"

"This is the clever scripting that displays emails rather like an Internet page. One's friends and acquaintances rarely, if ever, construct colourful emails. They usually just type something. As a rule, only the commercial enterprises and the scammers send out HTML emails."

I think Holmes could see that he was beginning to lose me or perhaps it was the rumbling of my stomach.

"And why, of course, is this important? Because these HTML emails can transmit directly back to the sender, alerting them to your presence."

"My head above the parapet again?"

"Indeed. Also, the simple act of loading an image in such an HTML email can equally result in the activation of a malicious program."

"And what of the anti-virus programs, Holmes? Surely, they step in at this point?"

"In an ideal world they do, Watson. They should catch most of the culprits, but all attachments should be scanned with Avast before being opened if ever there is the faintest hint of suspicion. Luckily, most anti-spyware programs will spring into action in the majority of cases but I doubt if even they can catch such a slippery character as FinSpy."

We watched as our glasses were eventually refilled. I tapped them briefly together and took a lengthy sip.

"One thought does strike me, Holmes. In the Bahrain example, if my anti-virus programs are of no help and yet I still have a burning desire to learn more about the arrest, what might I do?"

"In this instance, dear chap, you should email Melissa using the address on her business card or company Internet site and confirm if she has sent you anything. After all, Watson, lives are at stake."

"Yes, I can see that would be worth the effort," I agreed. "But if they were thwarted that time around, surely these FinSpy people would simply try another approach?"

"Yes, you are right. Again, Watson, they are only limited by their imaginations and their victim's incredulity." Holmes helped himself to a handful of nuts from the silver dish on the counter. I swiftly did the same.

"One of their most popular wheezes is to send the victim a notification that the operating system on their smartphone needs to be urgently updated for security reasons. What then, Watson?"

"Well, I am assuming that such important updates are par for the course. I've had those, too. If it looked like it was coming from Apple then I would probably do as they ask."

"And you would be a fool to do so, Watson. Any such notification can be easily faked by anyone with a good graphics program. But, first of all, never accept any update that just pops up. If you need to update a program or operating system there will be a clear indication within your *Settings*. Only ever update that way."

Just then a flunky came over to Holmes and spoke quietly in his ear.

"Our table awaits," announced my friend, slipping from his barstool. "I hope you have worked up a good appetite. Bring your drink."

We were led to our usual table, so advantageously placed that Holmes had a clear view of all the points of entry and exit within the splendour of the neo-Byzantine dining room. While we waited for the menus, my friend nodded towards my inside, left-hand breast pocket.

"This will amuse you, Watson. Go to Google Images and type *finspy* + *laptop* + *tape*. What do you see?"

"Right you are. Here is a rather swarthy fellow in a dark shirt." I peered closer at the photograph. "I see he has the word 'FinFisher' on the screen of his laptop. Any relation?"

"None other than the parent company of the malicious FinSpy," Holmes declared. "And the chap you see there is the big boss of the company. He might be very good at hoodwinking people into letting him plant nasty spy programs into their devices but he can never be so sure that he is not a victim himself."

"How can you tell, Holmes?"

My friend leaned close and enlarged the image on the screen. "Ha," he declared. "What have we here? It is tape once again."

"So people cannot look at him?"

"And yet he might sweep his laptop with all the smartest anti-spy programs but – so good is his product, a veritable weapon of war – that even he cannot adequately protect himself."

"Shocking."

"What do you say to our sharing a dozen of the delightful rock oysters?" Holmes leaned forward with an eager smile upon his sharp features.

I had to think twice as oysters were dashed expensive at that time of year. "The *pâté* is very good," I suggested. It was just then that Luigi our usual waiter came and handed us the menus.

"The lamb is especially good today," he addressed Holmes. "Whitstable salt marsh."

Holmes nodded for my approval.

"Could I have mine not so pink this time, Luigi?" said I.

"Of course, sir."

"We shall start with a dozen oysters, Luigi, and a bottle of the '02 *Montrachet*." Holmes turned and smiled at me. "Should go very nicely."

"Are we celebrating something, Holmes?" I felt as if on unsure ground.

"You are only just beginning to get the colour back in your cheeks, dear Doctor. A satisfying and nutritious luncheon should ensure your complete recovery."

"Very thoughtful of you, too, I must say, Holmes."

"Do you use Twitter?" he suddenly asked.

"I do dabble, I must admit. I have twenty-seven *Followers*. I like to maintain a select circle of *Tweeters*."

"Probably very wise, Watson. But do you ever receive notifications from people outside of your circle?"

"All of the time."

"And do you find Twitter helpful as a source for news?"

"Of course. Many people rely upon the social media outlets for their news nowadays. Facebook is a popular source, I understand, as is Twitter, especially for breaking stories."

"Quite so, Watson. But herein lie further traps. Imagine this, you are in your practice at Queen Anne Street. It is a bit of a slow day when – suddenly – up pops Twitter alerting you to a terrorist atrocity on the far side of the city. This is a BBC News Alert. There is a link allowing you to learn more. What do you do, Doctor?"

Just then the sommelier glided alongside Holmes and displayed the bottle for his approval. Several minutes later and I was enjoying the nice honey note that was brought out especially well in the '02 due to the light frost that year. "Where were we?" I had to ask.

"The terrorist event…"

"Yes. Right. I need to know the extent of the carnage. How many people are injured, how many reported killed so I can get an idea of scale. Even what kind of explosive or device has been deployed. I would try to get the precise location. Then I would grab my bag and hail a cab as swiftly as I could."

"And all very commendable, Doctor. But I am sorry to tell you that you might have just walked straight into another trap and taken yourself off into unsafe territory, and I do not mean Whitechapel."

"How so?"

"Because it is simplicity itself to stunt up a Tweet. Allow me to demonstrate." Holmes indicated my iPhone. "Go to your preferred search engine, Watson, and type *"lemme tweet that"* then follow the link. You will see a box in the centre of the page. Where it says *@EnterUserNameHere*, tap the screen and type *@BBCNews*."

I did as he bid and then peered incredulously at the screen. The page had transformed itself into the official BBC Twitter page. "Are you suggesting, Holmes, that I can now type into the box I see open before me and that somehow I will be creating a phoney BBC News Alert?"

"Precisely, Doctor. And then all one needs do is have it re-Tweeted and there it is, out there in the open."

"But what is the ultimate aim, Holmes?"

"The Drive-By Download, Watson. This phoney Tweet will take you to an equally phoney news page and there, as I have previously stated, you quietly and unobtrusively take on-board a malicious program much as you would the homely Cookie."

"And then they have me, I suppose?"

"They do, my friend." Holmes sat back in his chair, rising imposingly. "Ah, the oysters. They do look good, do they not, Doctor?"

"Succulent, I must say."

"Dive in, Doctor," said my friend, selecting an especially plump specimen and squeezing on lemon. He tilted back his head and gulped down the bivalve entire.

Holmes smacked his lips. "Sick, twisted individuals use real-life breaking news stories to jump on the bandwagon and draw unsuspecting victims off to their lairs for immediate infection," he explained.

"They can easily plant all manner of nasties – not just the old RAT – but Blackhole Exploit Kits with Trojans, backdoors, key-loggers, infostealers or rootkits. They might even load you up with the increasingly popular dodge of Ransomware."

I selected my second oyster, marvelling at the delicate translucency of the anterior *adductor* muscle. "Yes, I have heard of this," I said. "One's computer or 'phone is locked until you pay a ransom."

"Correct, Doctor. This may take many forms." Holmes polished off another oyster, leaving just two remaining on the platter. He smacked his lips once more and pressed on.

"The perpetrator of the intended crime might come straight out in the open and immediately strong-arm you for the cash, or they might pretend to be some official body, such as the police, accusing you of downloading illegal content and locking your device until the 'fine' is paid."

Holmes stretched forward and swiftly despatched another oyster. "Sometimes they include a mug shot of the victim taken as you might suppose, my friend, using the victim's very own webcam. That is rather disquieting, is it not?"

I agreed. "But is all lost, Holmes? Is one left with a dead device or must one pay up?" I looked forlornly at the singular oyster resting in its' juices. Holmes indicated that I should avail myself.

"Only a fool would do so, Watson. But not surprisingly the victims are legion – from actual police forces through to government departments and not just the dim-witted. It is fair to say that globally millions fall prey every year to these tricksters. And – by-the-by – Ransomware programs are easy to be had, meaning that any scoundrel can take up this scam."

My friend sat back, allowing Luigi to clear away our things. He then lightly dabbed his lips with the napkin and, as soon as we were on our own again, he pressed on in a low voice. "Needless to say, once the ransom is handed over – usually by Western Union or sometimes via a digital crypto currency such as the BitCoin – the machine stays locked."

"So one is scuppered then, Holmes." I dabbed my own lips.

He chuckled. "But the key here, dear fellow, is not to fall victim in the first place, not to open an attachment or willy-nilly follow a link."

"I suppose not."

"Regardless of who wants you to follow a link – be it some global news monolith or even your Mum – always look at the address first. If it is obviously from the BBC with the corporation's legitimate Internet address, all well and good. But often it is a shortened link, some gobbledegook that looks like a meaningless jumble of letters. Now you have no idea where you are going."

"I suppose not," I said again.

"The answer, Watson, is to expand the link. To see it fully naked, to see where it intends to take you."

"And how, pray?"

Holmes nodded to the iPhone that lay beside me, reflecting back the splendid gold ceiling. "Search *expand + short links* and, with a little cut and paste, the true address will be revealed."

"But if one were imbecilic enough to fall for this one, then what? Is it ever too late?"

"There may still be a chance, Watson. As quick as you can, switch off your computer and then back on again. On start up, a user is often presented with two options, to login as oneself or as a guest."

"Yes, I have that on my laptop."

"So, Doctor, you must now login as the guest. If luck is on your side, you can recover your important data via this route."

Holmes raised his right hand to underline his next point. "One should really use a detachable storage device as the prime stowage facility and backup from that into the regular machine, rather than the other way around."

"Oh, I see."

"That way," explained Holmes. "Even if they have total control of your computer, my friend, you can simply unplug the storage device and access it from another machine. Your data will not be lost."

"What a relief, Holmes." I exclaimed. "But one's computer is then *kaput*, I take it."

Holmes gave his sardonic chuckle. "There is still one avenue that a victim might explore. If all else fails, Watson, go online using another device and search for *No More Ransom*. If anybody can solve your problem they can and it's free."

Holmes sat back gleefully. "Ah, the lamb."

"My dear Doctor you positively inhaled that sticky toffee pudding," marvelled Holmes.

I sat back in my chair. "Well, I did not find the oysters especially filling and, as you know, I am not partial to bloody lamb."

"Ah, but lamb cooked in the French manner is sublime."

"Holmes, if you had spent as much time as I dressing open wounds you might prefer it well done."

Holmes nodded his understanding and I took a sip of my coffee. In time Luigi trotted up and slipped the bill on the table between the two of us.

"We have not yet covered industrial espionage," announced Holmes as he unwrapped an after-dinner mint. "All corporations, as you no doubt know, have their own in-house intelligence services these days. They want to know what their competitors are up to and they want to keep a close eye on their employees. And when it comes to being spied upon themselves, they like to think that they are bottled up tight."

"So I imagine." I looked at the leather folder that lay between us. I remember thinking that the second bottle of *Montrachet* had been something of an extravagance.

"If you think, Watson, most of these entities maintain firewalls and teams of technical people on alert for any form of penetration. Any corporation on the ball will be locked down good and proper."

"So dodgy email attachments and phoney Tweets may not do the job, eh?"

"That side of things is fairly well sewn up, Watson."

"So what can a penetrator do?" I struggled to keep my eyes on Holmes, their being drawn to the folder with the growing concern that I was expected to make the right move here.

"Here is a scenario for you. You work in a big office in the City. You often pop out for a quick bite to eat at a nearby sandwich shop where you may occasionally linger over a *cappuccino*." Holmes drained the last of his own coffee.

"One day, you notice a small USB thumb drive lying on the floor under your table. You nudge it with your foot and see that there is a sticker attached bearing the word 'Private'. What do you do, Watson?"

"Well, Holmes, as you know, I am not one to pry. If something is private then in my book it should stay that way but I see where this is going. I might, in the first instance, go and hand it in at the counter."

"Excellent, Watson, if the target here were the sandwich bar – but it is not."

"For the sake of your narrative, Holmes, I will take it back to my office and plug it into my computer. I will hope – I suppose – that the thumb drive contains pornography of an especially private and lurid nature."

"And so would many people, my friend. That is one way in. You might just as easily drop the thumb drive on the floor in the corporation's lobby."

"It's a bit like fishing, only the other kind," I suggested.

Holmes leaned forward again. His hand was nearly touching the folder and its' potentially alarming tally. "Here is another scenario, Watson." As he sat back in his chair, the folder appeared to move marginally in my direction.

"You are the receptionist working in that lobby. An attractive, well presented young lady arrives at your counter. She is clearly distressed."

"Dear me."

"She needs your help, Watson. She has a vital job interview in less than thirty minutes. But, alas, she has contrived to spill coffee all over her presentation. *Oh, golly*, she says. *I've ruined my presentation, what am I to do?*"

"Is she a *little* girl, Holmes?"

"No, dear chap, she is in her early twenties. I shall continue. *"Please Mister*, she implores. *I have a copy here in this USB thumb drive. If only there were a printer somewhere.*"

"Yes, yes, Holmes. I get the picture. I will play the perfect gentleman and make a copy for her using my printer."

"So very kind of you, Watson. Believe me this is a scam that is played out in countless variations every day. And – as I am sure you already suspect – a covert piece of spyware waiting in the USB will immediately infect the computer at reception which in turn will infect the entire network."

"But what about these computer geeks guarding against penetration?"

"They are fully occupied, eating pizza and looking in the wrong direction. They are inside, looking out while our attractive trickster has wormed her way inside. Trust me, nine times out of ten this simple ploy will work."

Holmes lifted an eyebrow and caught Luigi's immediate attention. He reached into his trouser pocket and extracted a tidy wad of banknotes held in place by a silver money clip. He then slipped a selection of notes into the unopened folder.

"Are you not going to look at the bill?" I asked.

Holmes was already standing. "I am fully capable of keeping a running count. Your shout next time, Doctor."

"It's comin' down cats and dogs good and proper out there, Mr 'olmes. Should you like me to call you a cab, sir?"

"You may have a deuce of a job on an afternoon like this, William," said my friend. "We shall be in the Long Bar."

We were enjoying a simple brandy apiece up against the counter when Holmes indicated a point across my shoulder. "Don't look now, Watson, but I happen to know that the fellow in the Gieves & Hawkes suit is the Chief Executive Officer of a long-established merchant bank. I also happen to know a little something of the man's interests."

"Such as?"

"That he is an incorrigible philatelist with a particular interest in stamps featuring early aviation."

"Fascinating."

"But this is the way in, don't you see?" whispered Holmes. "If we were out to penetrate this long-established merchant bank, the man behind you is our perfect method of penetration."

"How so?"

"We would begin by searching him high and low across the social media spectrum. We would join our own dots and discover his particular hangouts. I imagine he might be a visitor to any number of popular philately forums and discussion rooms."

"I see."

"Knowing his particular interest, I would offer up for sale something irresistible – a rare German New Guinea two-pfennigs Blue featuring a *Graff Zeppelin*, for instance. I would go phishing for our man."

"You cannot put the virus in the stamp, can you Holmes?"

"No, my dear friend, but I can plant my spy tool inside the very photograph that I post on the forum, ready to activate the instant the image is enlarged. With our friend the RAT, I can physically watch every interested party via webcam. I throw back all the tiddlers until I have our particular big fish."

Holmes was looking over my shoulder again. "From then on, dear fellow, I have access to all his emails, texts, online banking and what-have-you. I can ask to have passwords reset at my command. My options are boundless."

"Mr 'olmes, sir. Your cab is 'ere."

"Well done, William." Holmes fished in his pocket. "Here is something for your trouble."

"Oh, thank you very much, sir. I just wanted to say again 'ow grateful my missus and me are, sir, you 'elping resolve that issue for us, Mr 'olmes."

Holmes waved his gloved hand airily and smiled before turning to me. "Sorry old chap. Must dash."

CHAPTER SEVEN
The Drawbridge

"Very good of you, Holmes, to invite me along for the ride."

"How could I not, dear fellow? After all, I have heard you reminisce about Chomply Saint Anne's countless times over the years."

I looked with pleasure out of the window at the green and occasionally bright yellow pastures that sped by. For once the skies had cleared, casting a pale and watery evening illumination upon the fields.

"Do you suppose that it has changed much, Holmes?" I pondered. "It was once the finest market town in the entire Garden of England. Chaucer gives it a mention."

"So I believe."

"I caught my first trout in the brook beside the old Norman church." The train rattled along. The thick verdant greenery of the passing embankment gave me the childlike sensation of travelling back through time down a hazy and melancholy tunnel.

"I believe you spent your school holidays with your mother's eldest brother, is that not right, Watson?"

"Good Old Uncle Henry." I had to chuckle. "He has the Manor House, or rather he did have. It would be interesting to see the old place again, to see who has it now."

"We may find the time yet."

"I had my first-ever pint in the Bull Inn," I smiled at the memory.

"Now there is an idea, old chap."

"Then I have the perfect hostelry for you, Holmes," I enthused. "Horse brasses everywhere. Nice roaring fire. Old Charlie Lavender – his face a mass of whiskers – propping up the bar in the corner and nursing his stout. The ever-jovial Archie Marley pulling the pints."

"Good food, Watson?"

"The best. Lovely rich pies. A jugged hare I shall never forget, Holmes."

My friend consulted his watch. "Then brace yourself, Watson. Chomply Junction in two minutes."

I stood aghast as Holmes referred to his Android. "Right we are, Watson. Turn left out of the station, count the kebab shops on the right-hand side until we reach the third one and our Airbnb apartment is just above."

"Holmes," I shook my head. "Holmes?"

My friend rested a firm arm across my shoulders and peered down at me. "Just my little jest, Watson. There is only the one kebab shop. Let us press on so we can dress for dinner."

"I am reliably informed, Watson, that the Bull Inn is now a franchise operation within the Witherspoon Corporation pub chain. I imagine, also, that both the redoubtable Charlie Lavender and ever-jolly Archie Marley are long gone."

"I should hope so, too."

"Cheer up, old chap. Get this down you." Holmes placed two foaming pints onto the table. "Old Speckled Hen. Good head, I must confess, and surprisingly inexpensive comparatively-speaking."

Holmes drained the first four inches and sank back into his alcove bench seat while his beady, bird-like eyes absorbed every detail of our sterile environment.

Some time later, after our unassuming repast was at an end, Holmes and I settled down to examining our respective smartphones. In time, my friend delved within his Inverness cape and extracted his notebook computer which is even more compact than my own iPad Air Mini.

Time passed and then, suddenly – as if from almost nowhere – Holmes vehemently declared, "Confound that whining music; it gets on my nerves."

Often, one is only aware of a background sound once it stops. This happened now. The depressing *muzak* came to an abrupt finish. The room was suddenly basked in silence the way a room suddenly might be when one utters a stupid remark and everybody instantly turns and looks at you.

Holmes had a self-satisfied smirk to his sharp, chiselled face.

"Am I missing something, Holmes?" I asked.

Rather than answering my question directly, my friend leaned across the table and held the screen of his notebook up for my inspection. "Here is a suspicious fellow if ever I saw one," declared Holmes. "What do you make of him, Watson?"

"If anything," I peered close. "He is over-weight, his hair is receding which may be an indicator of a stressful life as well as advancing age. He has an air of the woebegone about him. Who is he, Holmes, and should I care particularly?"

"Care, Watson." Holmes came over all mysterious and nodded his head backwards and upwards. I followed his directions but remained nonplussed.

My friend leaned closer now and lowered his voice. "Act nonchalant, old chap, but we are in control. Watch this." Holmes grasped back his notebook and flicked repeatedly at the screen.

"These are the toilets, Watson. I am not entirely sure if this is legal." He held the screen up. I was looking at a row of urinals and a person in a 'hoody' who was obviously the worse for wear. I gave Holmes my flummoxed face.

"The Wi-Fi router, Watson. I am 'in' and now I have total control. You see that camera up there in the corner? Give a wave. Smile for the camera."

And, of course, the penny eventually dropped. I was the woebegone fellow with the receding hairline. I felt violated. Suddenly I wanted to be at home in my own bed but I had to play along for form's sake.

"Good heavens, Holmes," I declared. "Are you hacking and – if so – how in the name of all that is good have you managed such a thing?"

"Simplicity itself, my dear fellow. In this instance I have logged in to the free Wi-Fi whilst forgoing any VPN such as Hotspot Shield as I wish to identify the Internet Protocol Address at this location."

I sighed inwardly and enacted a theatrical yawn that failed to deter my friend now he was on 'a roll'.

"See here, Watson, I am employing the Angry IP Scanner, a free and open-source program for all operating systems. Armed now with one local IP address, I allow the program to seek out other addresses within a certain range and, behold, there are many."

I had to agree.

"I am looking for connected devices that have not been secured, those with open ports. You would be astounded, my friend, to learn that very few people ever bother to institute basic security and change the password on their Wi-Fi routers or connected devices. Let me show you how I can now control the cameras."

Holmes tilted the screen allowing me a better view. "Here we have a comprehensive list of all locally connected devices. I seek out the IP cameras such as the one pointing at you now."

Holmes stopped to quickly sup his beer. "Those marked with a green dot are open. I note their particular IP address, type it into any browser and up pops a box asking me to input the Username and Password for the camera."

"But you cannot possibly know the passwords, Holmes."

"I do not need to. I can look them up. I see here on the screen the precise make and model of that camera. I go to the manufacture's Internet page and look up the default password. In this instance, I type in *admin* for the username and *admin* for the password. See, I am now controlling the camera in the kitchen."

"Well, I am flabbergasted. You mean to tell me that these devices are wide open?"

Holmes chuckled. "Thanks to the general apathy of most people, combined with their limited technical know-how, so many connected devices are open to all and sundry."

I looked around the poorly-lit bar and realised that almost everyone was either updating their Facebook status or playing that amusing game with the chickens.

"We were fortunate in this instance, Watson, that we have stumbled upon just such a location. Be so good as to get in another round and when you get back I shall introduce you to the world's most dangerous search engine."

"Bishop's Finger," I announced placing two amber pints on the table and slipping back into my chair. "I think you have the bar staff in something of a tizz, Holmes. People are complaining that the music has stopped and everyone appears at a loss how to switch it back on."

"All in good time, Watson, but first I want to demonstrate the Shodan search engine."

"Fire away."

"Picture this, Watson. You are a spotty, solitary teenager new to the world of hacking. You do not have a specific target in mind but you want something easy – a vulnerable and easy to hack objective. It might be anywhere on the planet. Therefore, imagine if you had a search engine rather like Google but one that would help you seek out your first helpless victim. Welcome to Shodan."

"Really?"

"These days, Watson, you go to a shop and buy a new refrigerator. The chances are that it will connect to the Internet once you get it home. It will manage your groceries and even order up fresh supplies from your friendly online supermarket, such as Ocado."

"I've had the same fridge for over ten years," I huffed. "I had no idea these things were available, let alone even possible."

"Increasingly all modern products are becoming 'connected' and every one of these devices has its' own unique Internet Protocol Address, the IP address, and this is what Shodan searches for. If it is connected to the Internet, then Shodan will find it. It is then up to the hacker to seek out the vulnerable ones and have a little fun."

"Shocking, Holmes. But how is it that such a portentous tool is allowed to stay up there?"

"Because, my friend, much like everything else, it can be used for the purpose of good and for the purpose of evil. Developers uses Shodan to test vulnerabilities, keeping us all ultimately safer. It has many positive uses."

"But it just so happens to be a hacker's delight, eh?"

"Watson, Shodan is no more than a beautifully-indexed map of the known Internet. That is hardly a crime."

"Show me something nice, then?" I suggested.

"Bear with me, Watson." Holmes tapped frantically at the screen. He pulled up page after page. "This is a bird table in the Paddington district of Brisbane. See, I can zoom in and out and pan right and left. I believe this is a kookaburra."

"Very nice."

Holmes opened another page. "These are the security cameras for Boulder Municipal Airport in Colorado. Again, I can move the cameras around and zoom in and out. Look how deep that snow is, Watson. A picture postcard."

Holmes let out a sharp laugh. "And here, Watson, is why I recommend you tape up your computer camera. Here is the view from a person's webcam somewhere in Pretoria. We can see the living room stretching out to the darkened veranda and the stars twinkling in the distance over the *veldt*."

I shook my head. "You are making me feel rather queasy, Holmes. This is like having a RAT but without all the trouble of Social Engineering the victim."

Now Holmes yawned. "What say we finish our drinks and then head back to the apartment? We have a long day ahead of us."

"Yes, please." I knocked back the last of my pint and rose out of my chair. "My old Nan use to say 'bed is the best place' and I am inclined to agree with her, Holmes."

'So right she was, my friend."

"Ah," I announced while negotiating our way to the exit. "They have managed to get the music back on again."

"So they have."

"Can't imagine that *Das Rheingold* from Wagner's Ring Cycle would be their cup of tea."

"Is it too loud, Watson?" I had to strain to catch his words.

"Just a tad."

"This is Poppinghole Lane here, Holmes." I stood to catch my breath. "The old Manor House is about half-a-mile this way."

"I think I see it now, Watson. Up on the hill there." Holmes shaded his eyes from the low and sickly morning sun. "What a delight, and in the style of James Gibbs. Let us press on."

Some little while later Holmes and I came to an abrupt halt at the imposing entry gates. "Nobody at home it would seem," announced my friend.

"Are you sure?"

"Elementary. There are no motor vehicles on the drive. The manor is a considerable walk to the main road and I imagine that even domestic servants have their own cars these days."

Holmes nudged me gently. "Besides, the security cameras confirm my notion." He showed me his notebook's screen. He held it horizontally and I could see a bank of eight black and white monitors depicting the horseshoe-shaped driveway, the imposing entrance hall with sweeping staircase. There were bedrooms, bathrooms, utility areas and the old basement kitchen.

"There's more on this page," said Holmes.

"Holmes, please tell me that you have not hacked into my old summer home, the castle of my youth?"

"A piece of cake, too, Watson. Theirs is the only Wi-Fi signal for miles around. Given the thickness of the walls of this Georgian delight, they have been obliged to install numerous boosters. As luck would have it, they are employing a Netgear router. I do not even need to look up the password. I simply type *admin* as username and *password* as the password and we have breached the drawbridge."

"Holmes," I put in suddenly. "Watch out. Somebody is opening one of the blinds – up there."

But my friend just laughed. "What we have here, Watson, is a prime example of more money than sense. This entire house is part of the Internet of Things – the world of connected devices all with their own IP addresses. I can open and close the blinds. I can switch on the lights of an evening while riding the train home. All with a simple application on my smartphone. I can run myself a nice deep bath while sitting on the sofa and catching up with *Eastenders*."

"But do you have the necessary applications?"

"I do not need to, Watson, for I already have the main control panel in convenient HTML format here at my fingertips." He waged his notebook and the screen briefly reflected into my eyes.

"Holmes, we are intruding. I think we should leave now."

"Not on your life, Watson. I want to run a scenario by you."

I watched as the blind rolled back down. I looked briefly all around me and reluctantly indicated that Holmes should carry on.

"Visualise this, Watson. You are an attractive woman in early middle-age. You are in your delightful en-suite bathroom. The lights are low and emitting a calming pink aura thanks to the Philips HUE lighting system that can also be controlled by a smartphone app.

"You are luxuriating in a deep roll-top bath with some of the finest products of the Body Shop. You are alone. Your husband is away on business in Dubai and is not expected back until the weekend.

"The husband, who is in thrall to most new technology, has wired the house from top to bottom. Everything around you is connected to the Internet of Things. You have another sip of vodka and settle back in the bath, letting the suds crackle and pop about your ears.

"And then, Watson – all of a sudden – you are aware of a change. You cannot put your finger on it at first. Are the lights dimmer now? Are they no longer so pink and cheerful but rather grey and sinister? Is it you, Watson, or is it colder in the room now? You shiver and lower yourself deeper into the all-encompassing warmth of the bath water.

"Just then your Michael Bublé album being played out of the Bluetooth speakers cuts dead. The lights immediately go out. You could not even see your hand before your face. Then, Watson, ice-cold water bursts forth from the tap at your toes. You scream, Watson. You scream but nobody can hear you."

"Good heavens, Holmes. what are you getting at? I won't sleep properly for a week now."

Holmes slipped the notebook back in his pocket and pulled the collar of his cape tight around his neck as turned to me. "And the moral of this story, my dear fellow, is that people who do not bother to change the passwords on their connected devices – and in particular the home or office Wi-Fi router – are inviting every Tom, Dick and Harry to come spy upon them."

"Even so," I protested.

"Watson, there you are in a pitch-black, ice-cold room, immersed in freezing water that is now gushing over the roll-top at an alarming rate and you are immobilised and powerless.

"The lock to the bathroom door is also controlled by an app, should one wish. Now, Watson, the door clicks and clacks as if someone were trying to get in.

"Then, rather like a bad dose of tinnitus, the sound system is emitting a most distressing wail. It gets so loud that you are now deaf as well as blind and fast approaching paralysis from the sheer cold. What do you do, Watson?"

"Scream some more, Holmes. But is this a home invasion? If I were to get out of the bath and fumble for my robe, what might I encounter on the other side of the door?"

"Precisely, Watson. Is it some demented fiend in a terrifying clown mask clutching a pounding chainsaw or is it some pimply and insular youth somewhere on the other side of the planet having a little fun?"

"This is so utterly shocking, Holmes. I simply cannot imagine anything worse than people penetrating my personal fiefdom in such an underhand manner."

"Come, come, Watson. Comparatively-speaking, this is just the tip of the iceberg. Greater dangers lurk beneath."

We turned and began to make our way back down the lane.

"For reasons – which in future days will appear the height of foolishness – Watson, there is a comprehensive impulse to connect every single thing to the Internet."

"So I am learning, Holmes."

"Suddenly, we have cars that are controlled by AI, artificial intelligence. Every traffic light and security camera. But it gets worse than that. The very satellites circling above our heads are Internet connected. Power plants, nuclear and otherwise. The entire supermarket delivery chain, the cash that flows from the ATMs."

"We are leaving ourselves vulnerable."

"Indeed we are. All of these things can be hacked, Watson."

"And it is too late to wean ourselves off our dependence, I suppose, Holmes?"

My friend looked to the sky. Dark and ominous clouds were forming. Rain was already breaking out along the horizon, obscuring Uncle Henry's fine home in feathery drizzle.

"Two minutes ago, Watson, you witnessed what one acned teenager can do with a basic computer, a little skill and know-how, and an encrypted Internet connection.

"Now imagine what big government budgets can buy. Imagine what the Russians and Chinese are capable of. The Brits. The Yanks. Look what they and the Israelis did to the Iranian nuclear program with the Stuxnet virus. The world is changing, Watson."

I unclasped my umbrella and popped it open, allowing Holmes to stoop inside. From within our gloomy little tent, Holmes looked into my eyes with a fierce intensity.

"When Clausewitz remarked that 'war is the continuation of politics by other means' he had no idea that there was another element yet to come, Watson. To his sage observation we must now add the Internet – the twenty-first century battleground where a nation can be brought to its knees with the click of a mouse."

"I think we can just make the two-forty-three back to Town if we hurry." I picked up my pace.

CHAPTER EIGHT
Down the Rabbit Hole

The rain lashed the window-panes of the cosy sitting-room in Baker Street and outside the wind set up a dismal howling. Mrs Hudson had laid out a tray of cold roast beef with some bottles of beer. The fire had settled back to a toasty red glow and all was right with the world.

"Did you bring your laptop, Watson?" asked my friend, leaning back luxuriously in his armchair

I fished the case out of my bag and lifted it up for Holmes' perusal.

"I see you have foregone Apple on this occasion and opted for a very reasonable Sony VAIO employing the Windows operating system. Any particular reason for that?" he asked.

"Cost primarily. Apple Macs being dashed expensive. Is anything wrong with it, Holmes?"

"No, not at all."

"So far, Holmes, our little foray into the digital world has left me unsure of myself and feeling generally troubled."

"In what way, Doctor?"

"I should have thought that was obvious, Holmes." I opened the screen and called up a new *Word* Document. "You have demonstrated just how simple it is for any of us to be spied upon – by governments, the corporate giants, the criminals and the insane – not to mention fleeced for cash at every turn and generally interfered with."

"Quite so."

"But I must confess, Holmes, that this whole affair has left me feeling violated and ill-prepared to venture out into the Internet again."

My friend stood upright and laughed. "Take stock, Doctor," said he, placing a large hand upon my shoulder. "We have identified those that threaten us. We are alert to their tricks and ploys. Now it is time to turn the tables, to put ourselves out of harm's way by being invisible to them."

"Right you are, Holmes." I returned to my VAIO, somewhat relieved.

"Which browser do you employ on your laptop there?" indicated my friend.

I had to quickly check as I had no idea up until then that there was any great difference between them. Finally I declared, "Microsoft Explorer."

"Forget it," said Holmes. "You can't remove it, so just leave it alone except to say you should use it only occasionally for very simple things like checking the headlines and looking up recipes."

"So what should I do?"

"These days, Watson, many people are concerned about the lack of privacy online. They are perturbed by this web of countless radiations that penetrates our lives from cradle to grave. Therefore, we must concentrate on selecting the right tools from the right people. Again, these are generally free and open-source. We must begin with the browser."

Holmes took a few lengthy strides until he was looking out of the window. "Adding, of course, that we have already installed anti-virus protection because what follows now adds a belt to our braces."

"Got you."

"For your all-important browser, Watson, you must install something less intrusive and more security conscious. I recommend Mozilla Firefox and it works on all systems."

I set to immediately. "Installing now, Holmes." I declared.

"We are going to get a little technical now, Watson, but – as before – nothing that you cannot handle. Let us begin with the Firefox *Settings*." Holmes crossed the room and leaned over my shoulder.

"Look for the Firefox logo in the corner. Select *Options/Options*. Here we now see a small dialog box. Open *Privacy*. Now tick the option *Tell websites I do not want to be tracked*. Also untick *Accept cookies from sites*. This will keep basic Cookies out of your system."

"Sounds good, Holmes." I clicked away.

"Under *Security*, tick *Warn me when sites try to install add-ons*. Remove all exceptions. Tick *Block reported attack sites*. Tick *Block reported web forgeries*. This will guard against Drive-By Downloads. Now untick *Remember passwords for sites* – for obvious reasons."

I acted as Holmes prescribed. "Continue," I finally encouraged.

"On the *Advanced* tab, under *General* tick *Warn me when websites try to redirect or reload the page*," nodded Holmes. "Under *Network* tick *Tell me when a website asks to store data for offline use*. This will limit your appearances in databases."

"Sorted."

"On your new browser, Watson, you have a *Private* viewing option. Click in the top right-hand corner. You are looking for the *Menu*. Now select *New Private Window*." Holmes stepped back into the centre of the snug living room.

"Ah, ha," declared I. "I now see here a purple-coloured page with the words *Private Browsing with Tracking Protection*. What are its' benefits, Holmes?"

"One's browser, dear fellow, will give away all the important details of a person," said Holmes.

"The normal browsers store everything you do – from your downloads, what pages you visit, which chat rooms, the photographs you upload, together with the when and for how long each time. Not to mention all the passwords and location data. This is all grist to the databases, Watson, the State snooping and targeting advertisements."

My friend began to look around the room, on the prowl for an amusing distraction. He finally turned back to me. "The less information you have on your browser, Watson, the safer you are – especially if somebody were to sneak about."

"I imagine, Holmes, that this *Private* facility would be especially useful in a family situation where more than one person has access to a particular device. A person might accidentally login to another's Facebook or Twitter account in the ordinary course of events."

"Precisely, old chap. This way your Internet session is wiped clean the instant you close the Firefox *Private* browser."

I nodded understanding.

"Just suppose that you were buying a Christmas present for your delightful new friend. In the absence of *Private* browsing, she might be on Amazon looking for some Liz Earle make-up when she stumbles upon your activities, rendering all element of surprise adrift."

"Good gosh, Holmes. I hadn't thought about that."

"And that is why, Watson, in some circles this facility is known as the *porn portal*."

Holmes suddenly made directly for the violin case. I had just enough time to clamp my jaws tightly shut before he began a laborious draw on the bow, setting the china to rattle on the shelf. He speedily came and seated himself once more.

"Another benefit of Firefox, old chap, are the free add-ons one might attach. One essential is *DownThemAll* which allows a person to download a thing whilst keeping all of his security settings in place. It can also speed things up a bit, too."

"And where might I get that, Holmes?"

"There is only the one place for add-ons, Watson. Search *firefox* + *add-ons* and take your pick from within the Mozilla domain. There are free apps here that block advertisements as well as Cookies, and many privacy and security applications, including *Blur* which issues an alert whenever someone attempts to track you."

Holmes closed his eyes and scrapped carelessly at the fiddle which was thrown across his knee. "And, old fellow, we must not forget to mention search engines."

"I was wondering when you might get to that, Holmes. You appear to sneer at the mere mention of Google."

Holmes cackled and scratched a sour note. "Yes, old boy, I do have an aversion to search engines that store every question one asks and then makes that data available to the commercial world or to tools of the State upon request and without the benefit of a court order."

Holmes scrapped some more. "Besides, there are plenty of equally good alternatives that will not keep any record of your activities. I favour duckduckgo.com – probably because I like the name."

Holmes stroked some more at his fiddle, conjuring up flocks of migratory geese bound for warmer climes.

"If one were serious, my friend, one would altogether ditch the Microsoft programs that came bundled with your machine. They leak like sieves."

"Really?" I wondered, looking down at my screen and hazy notes.

"Stop using *Word* and go for the *Open Office Suite* – same thing, just costs nothing. Do not use *Windows Media Player*, search for *VLC media player* instead. And don't trouble yourself with Adobe's Acrobat Reader. It simply cannot keep a secret, so look up *Foxit PDF Reader* instead."

Holmes lifted his bow and began to scratch with it at a point on his neck before pressing on.

"And then, of course, one needs a reliable VPN – the old Virtual Private Network. Sad to say, Hotspot Shield – whilst ideal for mobile devices – is not suited to laptop or desktop computers. One must invariably push the boat out here and pay up a fee."

Holmes continued to scrape.

"But, Watson, I am loath to make a specific recommendation. However, that said, one should – in selecting a suitable VPN – ensure that you select one which does not hand over your data to anyone who asks, otherwise they are in no way 'anonymous'. The best bet is to search *recommended secure vpns* and, once again, take your pick. Got that?"

As I nodded confirmation, Holmes thankfully put the fiddle aside, sat back in his chair and crossed his legs with a decisive air.

"With a good VPN, Watson, one might pretend to be anywhere on the planet. Already we have gone a long way in shoring up our defences. With the VPN we obscure our identity and location."

"You have helped set my mind at rest," I assured my friend.

"Instead of sitting here in a cold, windy London, one might be in Tegucigalpa eating a spicy *baleada* and knocking back an ice-cold Port Royal in the shade of a lofty pine tree for all any inquisitive government spook or advertising algorithm might know."

"Got you, Holmes."

"What say you – my friend – to a bite to eat? Mrs Hudson has done us proud. And then, perhaps, we might take this up a notch and start applying some serious security measures."

I was just beginning to nod off when I was aware of a soft step on the stair and then a timid knock. Mrs Hudson pressed open the door and peered in at us. "Should you like me to clear up now, Mr Holmes?"

"If you would be so kind, Mrs Hudson. Did you bring my onion?"

"I have it right here, sir." She handed Holmes a small plate and paring knife and was careful not to let the onion roll off onto the floor.

As soon as we were alone again, Holmes began to examine the onion – turning it this way and that, as if his sheer willpower might penetrate deep within its papery skin.

"Watson, I would like to introduce you to *Tor* – The Onion Router." Holmes held up the large, reddish bulb. "We are about to enter the world of Hidden Networks, the other Internets that I have spoken of."

I roused myself and sat up in my chair, showing Holmes that he held my fullest attention.

"Onion routing is a technique for anonymous communication over a computer network, Watson. In an onion network, messages are encapsulated in layers of encryption, analogous to layers of an onion."

"In layman's terms please, Holmes," I bid.

My friend assented and held the onion firmly in one hand and, by use of the paring knife, cut deep into its milky white flesh.

"Be careful not to hurt yourself, Holmes," I cautioned.

Holmes pulled the onion into two separate halves and showed them to me.

"Think of each layer – each individual skin – as a separate layer within the Internet. When your encrypted message hits a new layer, there are so-called 'network nodes' that peel back the layer allowing you to pass through. The layer then reseals itself."

Holmes placed one half of the onion on the rug at our feet and then stabbed gently into the remaining half in his hand.

"The data that you send – any request from your computer – passes through multiple levels until it reaches its destination," explained Holmes, tunnelling the knife deeper into the flesh.

"As you arrive at each new layer, that node only knows the layer to either side of it. It cannot tell where your request came from nor where it is ultimately going."

I gasped. "This is all so fiendishly complicated, Holmes. But, if I understand you correctly, then the signal that I send is masked in the manner of a curtain at every waypoint along its journey."

"Yes, my friend, you have grasped the concept neatly. And each one of these nodes might be anywhere on the planet. Your request is bounced around like a tiny silver ball in a global arcade machine."

"That is rather a lot of analogies to take in all in one go, Holmes," said I. "But how might I use this onion network and how did it get there in the first place?"

"If you think back, Watson, the original aim of the Internet was to provide a means of communication in the event of a nuclear war. It worked by connecting hundreds of computers together and – if any part of that network went down – messages would automatically re-route to the remaining computers."

"Vaguely."

"Well, my friend, once they had that up and running, it was only natural that the spies, the military and the diplomats would want their own secure Internet. Thus, Tor was born." Holmes gave a little chuckle.

"In time, of course, word got out and now all sorts – journalists, aid workers, human rights activists and criminals, of course – use Tor for their secure communications and other secret online activities."

"And how does one enter this onion network?"

"You recall the Firefox browser that you configured before lunch? Well, I have something very similar for you – and once again it is free and open-source. Search *tor + firefox bundle* and set it up the way you did earlier, being sure to include the same add-ons as before."

Holmes got up from his chair and began to scout around the room again while I set about downloading and setting up the Tor browser.

In time, a pale green-coloured page popped up on my screen bearing the words, *Congratulations. Your browser is configured to use Tor… You are now anonymous and free to explore the Onion Network or branch off to the Surface Web.*

"Looks like I'm 'in'," I declared, sitting back and marveling.

Holmes strode towards me and peered intently over my shoulder. I looked up at him, feeling rather pleased with myself.

"Watson, you now hold in your hands the most singular weapon within our arsenal. With this, my friend, you can safely mask both your identify and your location. Nobody need know who you are or where you are."

"Good heavens, Holmes. Is this to say that I am now truly invisible?"

"You are, Watson, but with certain provisos. Trust me when I say that absolutely nothing is one-hundred percent safe or secure. That said, if we apply our own layers of secrecy at every turn then we are dashed difficult to find."

"But is this not what the VPN is for?"

"So right you are, Doctor. But the VPN is just one of our multiple layers. From now on, whenever you activate Tor, be sure to activate your VPN first. That way your Internet Service Provider or anyone snooping on your network will be left in the dark. They will not even know that you are on the Tor network. You will have slipped under the radar."

"I see." I thought.

Holmes now leant across me and pointed to the top left-hand corner of my screen. "Click that 'S' symbol beside the Onion logo you see there, Watson. This is vitally important. Now select *Block scripts globally*. Well done. You are all set to go."

"And where shall we head, Holmes?" I asked expectantly.

"The Volunteer," announced my friend, taking me aback. "I detect a break in the rain. A few brisk steps and we shall have the change of scene that I now require."

The Volunteer was surprisingly busy for an early Tuesday evening. While Holmes pressed his way through the throng at the bar to order us a pint each of *Hacker Pschorr*, I located a quite table in the corner just as it was being vacated.

"Watson, you are a man of infinite resource," declared Holmes approving my choice of table some short time later. "Cheers."

We passed our time in pleasant conversation of the general sort. When I returned to our table with a fresh round in hand, Holmes leant towards me conspiratorially.

"Let us imagine now that you are a whistle blower, Watson. You have access to some terrible secret and you want the world to know about it but you don't want to get caught."

"Right you are."

"In an idea world, we would meet in a pub much like this, at a nice quite table and you would hand over your incriminating documents in an envelope." Holmes held up a boney and portentous finger.

"But that world has long gone, my friend. For starters, how would you arrange to meet a journalist, say, in the first place?"

I scratched my head. "I imagine in the old days I would ring the fellow up and arrange to meet him. But these days I would probably only get through to voice mail and waste my time. I might email him but I doubt if that would work either.

What should I do Holmes? I imagine I need something more cloak and dagger."

"So right you are, Doctor. Today's journalists are under permanent surveillance."

"Really?"

"But of course."

"You are talking of the intelligence services, I assume, Holmes."

My friend sat back in his chair and chuckled. "It is not just the intelligence agencies and law enforcement that today's hack should worry about, Watson. All kinds of people have a vested interest in knowing about the reporter's next story – individual criminals and criminal organisations, political parties and extremist groups, law firms and the corporate giants."

"Given their easily-had capabilities, Holmes, I imagine that these groups would be stupid if they did not."

"Precisely. Journalists have contact with politicians and activists, they have their finger on the pulse – one should hope – and they are capable of causing all kinds of trouble both to governments and to corporations. An adversary will monitor all his or her online activities and read their email. They will see who their contacts are and they will start to monitor them, too."

"Yes, of course." I helped myself to the open packet of crisps on the table. "So what are my options, Holmes?"

"Well, my friend, you might want to by-pass the journalist entirely, simply because the risks are too high."

Holmes' hawk-like eyes scanned the immediate area around our table. He lowered his voice. "Let us also assume, Watson, that you have the data in digital format somewhere."

I rubbed my chin and then declared, "Let us say that this data is on one of those tiny USB thumb drives."

"Now you are thinking, Watson. And this is where Tor comes in."

"I was hoping that you would get to that, Holmes."

"Tor has two prime functions. It allows you to travel the Surface Web with a very high degree of anonymity but it also works as a portal to the dark side."

"You are talking of the Deep Web or Dark Net that I keep hearing about, Holmes?"

"Precisely. Tor can take us to a parallel Internet much like the one you use every day with all the usual features. But this is a world hidden from view – way below the surface – and here you will find many secret discussion boards and anonymous file hosting sites."

"Really?"

"With a little bit of cut and pasting, you can upload vast quantities of text and images without leaving any trail back to yourself. You then post the link to the hosting site on a discussion board where lots of like-minded people will see it. Then, Watson, you can wash your hands of the whole affair, knowing that the terrible secret is now out there."

"What should I do with the thumb drive?" I asked.

"Throw it in the Thames. Burn it first or run a powerful magnet over it. Wipe off all fingerprints."

"But just suppose, Holmes, that the data were somehow on my computer. How might I dispose of it then? I can't just delete the thing, surely?"

"As luck would have it, Watson, there are plenty of free, open-source shredding tools. Get one with a good reputation, such as *Evidence Nuker*."

"But what say, Holmes, that I needed to get this data to a specific person? What might I do then?"

"I see. Let us assume that you want to approach a specific journalist and that you have her office email address. For obvious reasons, you will not be using your usual email. Use Tor now as your browser. Employ the VPN. Search on duckduckgo.com for an email re-mailing service such as the delightfully-named *AnonyMouse* and compose a message there. At the same time grab a temporary email address from the Icelandic company unseen.is."

—

I needed to pause my friend for a moment. "Re-mailer, Holmes?"

"Yes, Watson, just like regular email but these strip off any codes that might identify you and add new ones all along a torturously complex journey. When the email arrives at its destination, there is no way that it can traced back to you."

I was impressed.

"With this email, whet their appetite about the terrible secret – without naming any actual names or places – and enclose a link which takes them to an online self-destructing messaging system such as *PrivNote* where you can explain in more detail. At this stage, give them your new *unseen* email address."

"Self-destructing messages," I mused. "What an excellent idea."

"So they are, Watson. *PrivNote* is a free app that allows you to compose a message that will promptly self-destruct once read. *PrivNote* generates a link which you pass on via email or personal messaging. You can also ask *PrivNote* for a read receipt."

"I imagine, Holmes, that the sheer thought of a self-destructing message should have most journalists salivating."

"Correct. Now you have her attention, Watson, use another *PrivNote* to explain Tor if she does not know already and provide a link to the secret file store on the Tor network. You should also lock the document or file with a good password. Also, be careful how you name any document. Don't call it *Top Secret*. Give it the name of something that nobody will ever want to read, Watson. Call it *GrandmasGoatHeadSoup.doc* or *MyDissertation.PDF*."

"And if I wanted to communicate with her? If I needed to discuss terms or what-have-you?"

"Then use *PrivNote* or its Deep Web equivalent *NoteBin*. But keep moving around, keep changing email addresses, and ensure all messages are destroyed as you go."

"Could I not just send her an encrypted email? I hear that they are very good."

"You could, Watson. But herein lies yet another problem."

It was just then that Holmes drained his glass and indicated that I might catch up. He wiped his lips and continued, "Let us assume that you both have state-of-the-art encryption such as PGP – which stands for *Pretty Good Privacy*. You can look it up online."

"Possibly."

"The trouble is, my friend, that whilst encrypted messages cannot be intercepted and read in transit, they are none the less rather too conspicuous while they travel about. Agencies like the NSA and our own GCHQ scour the Internet for encrypted documents on the basis that if it is encrypted then somebody must be wanting to hide something."

"Why, of course they would."

"And if they were sufficiently interested, they can simply compel you to hand over your encryption keys – and all is lost."

"Suppose I did not want to hand over my encryption keys, Holmes? Suppose I demanded by basic human right to privacy?"

"Then they would laugh in your face, my friend. They would cite the war on terror and their new mandatory disclosure laws and oblige you to cough up your keys or face a similar penalty to that of carrying around an unlicensed firearm, such as our very own handgun."

"So I can forget encryption then, Holmes?"

"Not entirely, Watson. If everybody were to employ end-to-end encryption – meaning all their data were scrambled as it travelled around – then people like you and your journalist would not stand out from the crowd. Only when that day comes will encryption be truly safe."

"And can they break encryption?" I needed to know. I drained my glass and put it back on the table.

"I think that it is fair to say, Watson, that if the NSA could break the most sophisticated encryption, then the mathematical world would soon get to hear about it and then so would the rest of us."

Holmes was already out of his chair and urging me to follow along.

"So, my dear Doctor, encryption is fully capable of doing the job it is designed for and, to that end, it is generally secure. That said, we must only ever use open-source programs. There is no telling if the spooks have not put 'backdoors' in the products of the major corporations."

"What a tangled web to be sure, Holmes. And where are we off to now?"

Holmes took me by the arm. "Is it nearly eight o'clock and tonight is Wagner night at Covent Garden. If we hurry we might be in time for the second act."

CHAPTER NINE
An Inspector Calls

I experienced a sudden wave of annoyance when I stepped back into the living room in Holmes' Baker Street lodgings. The opera had left me feeling invigorated, washing away my cares and anxieties.

I was looking forward to a nightcap in front of the fire before making my weary way home. So imagine my surprise when we were greeted by a small and sallow, rat-faced, dark-eyed fellow sitting as happy as Larry in my otherwise inviting armchair.

"Ah, Inspector Lestrade," declared Holmes. "You received my message, then?"

"I did, Mr Holmes," said the Scotland Yard detective rising from my chair. "I assumed it must be important so I came at once."

"Very good of you, too, Inspector." Holmes slipped out of his cape and, shaking Lestrade briefly by the hand, made his way to the tantalus and unlocked his second best cognac.

A few minutes later and we were settled before the fire, a crystal snifter apiece and Lestrade looking at Holmes expectantly.

"I was hoping, Inspector, that you might be able to put Doctor Watson at ease," said my friend. "We were having a discussion earlier about terrorism and cyberspace and the Doctor here was rather concerned that the government were not doing nearly enough to ensure the safety of the public in these troubled times."

"Oh, I see," smirked Lestrade sitting back comfortably and crossing his legs. This, of course, was all news to me but knowing Holmes' devious methods I willingly played along.

"Well, Doctor, let me set your mind to rest," said the policeman in his furtive, sly manner. "We can be proud that this country leads the world in cyber security. We now have unprecedented surveillance powers allowing us to collect and intercept communications in new and inventive ways."

"But is it not true," said I. "That Edward Snowden has thrown the cat in among the pigeons and given the game away? Now everybody knows that the Americans and the Brits spy on the world at large and upon their own citizens to-boot. Have not the terrorists now 'gone dark' as a result?"

Lestrade studied his snifter and took a lengthy sip. "Well, Doctor, it is true to say that his reckless actions have seriously hamstrung my colleagues within the police and intelligence agencies. Many operations were ruined when the word got out and they 'went dark', as you say."

"Oh, dear," said I.

"Yes, our ability to track domestic and foreign crime gangs – including those relating to people trafficking – was reduced by about one-quarter; while cracking the communications of high-value national security targets took three times as long."

"Good gosh. Then Snowden's revelations were entirely news to these people, then?" I asked wide-eyed.

"No, not entirely, Doctor," said Lestrade in a condescending tone. "But the upshot is that the criminals *et al* have taken up more sophisticated measures, rendering it rather difficult for us to fight terrorism and combat serious crime, including child sex abuse, murder and drugs trafficking."

"Heavens," I declared. "But surely you are up to speed now and can tackle these felons?"

Lestrade narrowed his ferret-like eyes. "We have made great strides. In the old days it was just the post and telephones that we had to worry about. These days it's much more complicated and we have needed to move with the times, Doctor."

Lestrade swirled the last drop in his glass. "This has been a wake-up call," he said philosophically. "Since the traitorous Snowden, we now have new laws in place that compel the tech entities to hand over all possible data about a suspect. All service providers are obliged to store every tiny detail so we can call upon it as needs fit."

"I am impressed," I said in my most convincing manner. "Tell me more."

Lestrade chuckled. "We can force your Internet Service Provider to keep your Internet Connection Record – a list of services, messaging apps and the websites you use – for a full year now."

"But the service providers store this data do they?" I wanted to know. "Hopefully the cost is not to be born by the tax payer."

The policeman shook his head. "That is the beauty of the thing, don't you see? They hang on to it all – but they have to hand over anything we want when served with a notice"

"And all in the strictest confidence, I am sure," said I. "All safe and secure?"

"Secure as the Bank of England," smarmed Lestrade.

"I see," said I. "But just suppose, Inspector, that I were suspected of being up to no good. What tools are now at your disposal?"

"We would do everything vital to an investigation, Doctor. Technical data being the key to most modern-day criminal prosecutions. For starters, we would look at your mobile 'phone calls. We would look at the origin, location, destination and length of these calls. We would also do the same with your emails and text messages. We would want to see what you have downloaded and what videos you have been watching, as well as the websites you visited."

The Inspector looked to his empty glass and lifted his eyes towards Holmes. "We would also take a good squint at your contacts book and look into those people, too – and all the people in their contacts books. We would cast a wide net indeed."

"But surely you would not go to the trouble of monitoring all of them? Is it worth the effort?"

"A piece of cake, Doctor. We just need to call up their 'Bulk Data Sets' – basically, people's personal information files – such as medical records, political affiliations, sexual proclivities, the protests they attended, the books they read, their comments on websites and, obviously, their tax histories. All this can tell us a lot, you know. And, if needs be, we can dig a lot deeper into each individual."

Lestrade smirked as he tipped back his glass to ensure he had left not a drop behind. "On top of all that we can legally hack all your electronic equipment. We might covertly download the contents of your 'phone or remotely access your computer."

"The so-called RAT?"

"We don't like to use that term, Doctor."

Holmes – who was taking a back seat on this one – topped the policeman's glass but not as generously as before. He looked in my direction.

"But surely," I said, "The necessity of getting a court order or warrant can hinder an investigation when time is of the essence?"

"There you have it, Doctor. But that has been thought of already. These days even a mid-level police officer can give the go ahead for most operations. For the bigger stuff, certainly we need a judge or government minister, but it's basically just a rubber stamp job."

"I see."

"This give us the power to demand any data – not only for ourselves and the security services but for local councils, government departments and, of course, the tax man, too. All for the purposes of detecting or preventing crime. We have all the bases covered."

"And with stringent safeguards and robust oversight I imagine?" said Holmes.

"Of course."

"And what of encryption?" I wanted to know. "That must be tricky?"

"A thorn in our side up until now, I must say. But that, too, is not much of an issue any more. We can require telecommunications operators to remove encryption at our command," he said. "We can also force the suspect to give us his codes but we might not wish to give the game away too soon."

"But, unquestionably," I asked. "It would be much simpler if you just compelled the makers of these security products to include 'backdoors' in their products. You could keep knowledge of this a secret. That way no hackers could ever attempt to use the 'backdoors' themselves."

"I wish, Doctor," sighed Lestrade. "The current system is not perfect, sad to say. Our hope is that soon we can go one step further and oblige the designers of any operating system or app – be it for smartphone or desktop – to ensure we have access to all the data stored on that device."

"No hiding place," I marvelled theatrically.

"So right you are, Doctor. After all," he chuffed. "You can hardly expect us to find a needle in a haystack if we do not have total control over that haystack."

The policeman paused to laugh at his own joke before carrying on. "There should be no area of cyberspace which is a haven for those who seek to harm us, to plot treason, to poison the minds of the little children and peddle hatred under the radar."

"Then we can all rest securely in our beds tonight," said Holmes rising to his feet. He deftly relieved the Inspector of his empty glass. "Thank you so much for your time, inspector Lestrade. This has all been most informative but I know that you are a busy man."

"We shouldn't want to detain you a moment longer," I put in.

And with that, Holmes ushered Scotland yard's finest out of the door.

"That man is a buffoon," I declared the very instant we were alone again. Holmes topped up my snifter and I returned to my seat beside the fire. "I should think that George Orwell must be turning in his grave."

"Quite," mused Holmes coming to join me. "And one must ask what is the benefit in having these new laws except to legitimise the illegal practices of the past?"

"The very same that Snowden exposed," I chimed in.

Holmes sat back to nurse his cognac. "If they are trying to track down today's villains," he snorted, "then they are going the wrong way about it."

I had to agree. "Already, Holmes, I know how to mask my activities from the service provider and other snoopers. I can keep my browsing history off my computer. I know not to fall for their attempts to plant a rat. I can scramble my calls and send and receive secret messages."

"So you can," said my friend.

"If I did not know better, Holmes, I would say that this is just a pretext to spy on the public at large. And seriously," I exclaimed, "allowing the tax man the same legal snooping powers as the intelligence agencies just gives the whole game away."

I could see that Holmes agreed with me. "What sort of terrorist or criminal Mr big do they imagine that they are going to catch this way?" I wanted to know.

"Only the most hapless of terrorists and criminals of limited intelligence." Holmes drained his glass and rose to his feet. "Why not spend the night, my friend? Your old room is all made up. Mrs Hudson has laid out a fresh shirt and clean underwear."

"Good heavens, is that the time?" I declared eyeing the mantelpiece clock.

"Tomorrow, doctor, you shall require a clear head. It is time to demonstrate how today's tech-savvy terrorist and master criminal really operate – giving the likes of inspector Lestrade the complete run around."

"Right you are." I yawned.

"We also have kippers for breakfast."

CHAPTER TEN
Under the Radar

"I think we should get some air," declared Holmes.

I stood at the window agog at the thick fog outside. Swirls of grey vapour pushed slowly past, giving the distinct impression that I was riding the clouds in a warm and snug airship. The thought of venturing beyond the sitting room gave me the shivers.

It did not take long for me to lose my bearings once we were outside. Holmes kept up a brisk pace, turning left and right through the murky gloom with its almost total absence of traffic. Some time passed. I could discern the growing hubbub of a crowd.

I looked at Holmes, confusion no doubt writ large across my face. My friend just smiled enigmatically and led me on through the thick mist.

"Everybody has to move back. We have to give them space. Move back please."

"Where on earth are we, Holmes?" I tugged at my friend's cape in the gloom. A raucous female voice was penetrating the melancholy haze.

Suddenly I froze. My back went immediately rigid. From somewhere far off a sergeant-major was barking commands. Rifles clattered, boots clomped. And then from out of the impenetrable mist came the opening bars of that bouncy martial melody *The Liberty Bell March*.

"Good God, Holmes."

"That's right, Watson. We are at the Palace and just in the nick of time – the Changing of the Guard."

"We left the comfort of Baker Street for this?" I asked, perplexed.

Holmes looked down at me, his moist face shrouded in the mist. He laughed. "Not our ultimate destination, Doctor. But I thought this worth the detour."

We stayed and listened awhile, wrapped in our own solitary cocoon of swirling mist, the fife and drums of the Grenadier Guards sending further shivers down my spine. Holmes gently took me by the arm and soon we were walking across the soft, wet grass of St James's Park.

Eventually we came to a bench and sat down to rest our feet while two inquisitive ducks stared at us with deathly still from the grey vaporous waters of the lake.

Holmes turned and looked at me with a sharp intensity. His voice was low. "When US Navy Seals came for Osama bin Laden, Watson, the terrorist chief thought that he was hiding in plain sight. He thought that his large and yet unassuming compound in the Pakistan military town of Abbottabad would go unnoticed."

I looked at my friend.

"But in reality, Doctor, he was standing out from the crowd. He was making himself highly conspicuous."

"How so?"

"Because his was the only house in town that did not have a telephone line. It did not connect to the Internet and no mobile 'phones were registered to that address?"

"Yes, I see."

"He made the cardinal error, Watson, of 'going quiet' when what he should have done was give them something to monitor instead. If his house had been connected in the usual manner, he might have spent his days Tweeting about Harry Styles of the boy band *One Direction*. He should have been watching Bollywood musicals and posting ridiculous selfies of a fat, middle-aged man."

"And they would not have given his house a second glance," I mused.

"Precisely. And there is a lesson in this for all of us, my friend. One can never be certain that one is not being monitored. No matter how good your anti-spyware or how alert you are to their devious penetration methods, in the end they will always get in if they are determined enough."

I pulled the collar of my overcoat tight to keep out the damp

"Suppose, Watson, that you were an activist of some sort. Perhaps you have taken exception at plans to frack for gas in the midst of your picturesque country village. You have two adversaries – the corporation that wishes to frack and the organs of the State that work on the side of business in detriment to the actual wishes of the electorate."

"That would be shocking, Holmes."

"Oh, yes, and if they get wind that you are planning a protest of some sort, they will do their damnedest to thwart you, Watson. They will certainly want to get inside your digital devices – all of them. They will see your contacts, read your posts, texts and emails, bug your 'phone. They will know when you plan to stir things up in the village hall and they will be there, ready and waiting for you. What do you do, Watson?"

"Sell up while I have the chance."

"You throw them a googly, old chap. That's what you do. You give them something to monitor, to keep their attention diverted. You carry on as you always would, doing the things you usually do online. But you would keep your activism entirely separate. You would never use the same device and never from your home or office. You would operate in unexpected ways."

"And how might I do that, Holmes?" I wanted to know. But Holmes was already on his feet. He indicated that I should follow and once more we immersed ourselves in the thick mist.

"Very nice coffee, this," I told Holmes. We were sitting in the warmth of a coffee shop in an hotel somewhere on the other side of the park. Our coats had been taken off to dry and for the first time since leaving Baker Street I felt comfortable again.

"I have a present for you, Doctor." Holmes delved into his trouser pocket and produced a small black USB thumb drive. He placed it on the table between us and slid it towards me.

"And what's that then, Holmes?"

"It is the missing piece of the jigsaw, Doctor."

"A thumb drive?"

"Precisely. This one is thirty-two gigabytes which is ample indeed. I have installed on here everything you need to fight the good fight to save your village."

"Oh, really? What's on it, then?"

"First let me tell you how it should be deployed. Use this, dear fellow, exclusively for your activism. Simply slot it into any computer anywhere and you will not leave any trace of your activities behind on that machine. Everything that you do – from sending emails, posting photographs, reading blogs, downloading documents – will be handled by this secure USB."

"I am intrigued," I told him. "But please tell, what does it contain?"

"For starters, Watson, I have installed the Tor browser and a simple and inexpensive VPN. You plug in the drive, activate the VPN, then fire up Tor and you are ready to go."

"I see, but what if I wanted to write a document or crop a photograph. Surely I would need the computer for that?"

"Fear not, Doctor. I have also installed on here a micro operating system – effectively turning this tiny device into a computer in its own right. You have on here *Platform* from portableapps.com. It is free and open-source. Think of it much like Windows on your laptop. As soon as you switch on, you have everything you need at your fingertips just like a regular computer. You have your text editor, VLC Media Player, a photograph and graphics viewer, PDF reader, Avast Mobile, *DownThemAll*…"

"Just a second, Holmes. I am not taking notes. I did not come prepared."

Holmes chuckled. "Just remember to go to portableapps.com and download every conceivable tool that you think you need. But I have done this for you already, dear Doctor."

"One thought does occur to me, Holmes. You say this small, inexpensive USB thumb drive has been turned into a tiny computer in its own right, capable of doing all the usual things ones does on an expensive lap- or desktop?"

Holmes nodded.

"Well, this would be perfect for people on low-incomes in developing countries where they could not afford a computer of their own. Presumably, they could take it down to the local cyber-café and plug in and everything they need is held on this minuscule device – all their files, photographs and whatnot."

"So it would, Watson. A capital idea. You should spread the word."

Holmes indicated my cup. "Drink up, old chap. Time has come to try out your new toy. Let us make haste for this hotel's business centre where we can avail ourselves of an Internet-connected computer."

We tucked ourselves in at the far end of the room where nobody could look over our shoulders. I glanced up at Holmes, he nodded and so I pressed the USB drive into the slot on the machine beside me. Almost instantly up popped a dialog box. It identified itself as 'Susan'.

"Susan?" I asked.

"Why not?" shrugged my friend. "Now do as I told you. Initiate the *Platform* operating system, then click the VPN. Now Tor."

I did as he bid and soon the now familiar green Tor screen greeted me. I looked at Holmes for directions.

"Watson. Duckduckgo. Search *my IP address*. What do you see?"

"We are in Reykjavik, Iceland's capital, by all accounts," I smiled.

"You are now free, Watson, to travel the Internet doing anything you wish. Nobody knows where you are. They do not know who you are. You can watch what you like, you can read what you like and speak openly. You leave no trace." Holmes nudged me playfully in the side. "But put that aside for now. Close it down."

I shut down Tor and sat poised with my curser.

"Now my friend I want to introduce you to yet another Internet – a very different place entirely and one that predates your everyday Internet by many years."

Holmes pointed at the screen. "Activate *Newsbin*, Watson." I searched down Susan's list of applications and clicked the desired logo. A strange interface loaded.

"Have you ever heard of the Usenet Newsgroups, Doctor?"

I shook my head.

"Then you are not alone, my friend. Despite its colossal size, very few people even have a hint of its existence – which is strange given that so many people appear to use it."

"But what is it, Holmes?"

"The deepest mine imaginable. A rich seam of media files – photographs, music, the latest Hollywood blockbusters – that other people have posted and which you can download without drawing attention. It is also ideal for surreptitious communications."

Holmes turned to look at me. "Last night we heard that clown Lestrade talk of finding a needle in a haystack."

"Yes, and he said that in order to find the needle they needed total control over the haystack."

"Just so, and the man is a simpleton, Doctor. What we have here is not a single haystack but an entire universe of haystacks. And I venture to suggest that finding a needle down here is nigh impossible."

"So how does it work?"

"Usenet is rather like an immense bulletin board containing many thousands of individual groups. Anybody can post on any subject and anybody else can read those messages and download the attachments."

I scrolled down seemingly for miles.

"You need special Newsreader software – such as *Newsbin* – and a low-cost subscription to the network. It can be installed on any operating system, including a USB drive."

I had to put in, "But it doesn't look very exciting. Holmes. No flashy graphics and interesting pictures – just endless lists of things." I shook my head.

"Probably why it doesn't get the attention it deserves. The World Wide Web put an end to that with its nifty HTML pages."

"And is it safe?"

"Yes, Doctor. Usenet is secure if you take the right precautions. Again it is another rabbit hole that hides you from your service provider. Once inside, they cannot see what you are up to and especially so if you deploy a VPN beforehand and employ *DownThemAll* for the files you want."

"But what is all this? What are these groups?" I was still scrolling the page down.

Holmes sat back and took a deep breath. "If you can think of any subject, Watson, then there is a Newsgroup just for that. There are Newsgroups for things you have no idea about. If you have an interest in porcupines or were looking for a job in the aviation industry, then there is a group for you down here."

"I see."

"But today we are employing Usenet as a means of secret communication. Remember, Watson, you are an activist. You want to communicate with others in your group. You want your privacy."

I sat with my fingers poised above the keyboard.

"In the old days, Watson, you might place a cryptic notice in *The Times* to communicate with your group. Well, you can do that here. Messages can be sent and received by placing them inside any group you like – preferably the dullest possible."

I peered closer at the screen while continuing to scroll into the depths.

"By placing your message in a group devoted to the breeding of Airedale terriers, and giving it a title that nobody would every want to read – such as *Spam Buster Pro Amazing Discount* – you will have placed a needle inside the vastest of all possible haystacks that nobody without prior knowledge will ever be able to find."

I did have to chuckle, thinking of Lestrade and his bothersome and ill-placed superiority.

"But we can make it even harder for them, Doctor." Holmes pointed to the top of the screen. "In that search box, seek *alt.binaries.multimedia.erotica.asian*. Now search within that group for *An Lee Woo Prolapse*."

"Seriously, Holmes? Why would I wish to see that?"

"Precisely, Doctor. Why indeed would anybody? Have you found her yet?"

I pointed at the screen, careful to avoid fingerprints.

"Click download. Now back to Susan, my friend, and activate *OpenStego*."

"*OpenStego*?"

"Steganography, Doctor," explained Holmes. "The art of hiding things inside other things. This one is free and open-source. Use it now to locate An Lee in your downloads folder."

"I have it here in *OpenStego*, Holmes. This poor woman needs to see her doctor as soon as she can."

"So it would appear," nodded Holmes.

"She needs a full *anorectal* and *sigmoidoscopic* examination to evaluate the anal sphincters and to document any concomitant abnormalities in the rectum."

"I dare say," said my friend. "Now, do you remember our Pride password, Doctor?"

'With the number nine and capital M and W and the owl? Yes."

"Then when *OpenStego* bids you to enter a password, do so."

I pressed a few buttons and then – suddenly – An Lee's intussusception appeared to dissolve, leaving a text document in its place.

I sat there dumfounded. I looked at Holmes and then turned back to the screen. I mouthed the words silently with my lips. "*Bomb Kill Prime Minister Thursday*."

"And that, my friend, is just one way to communicate beneath the radar. That message might just as easily say *Meet Swan Inn Function Room 7pm Thursday* and your fracking adversaries would not have a clue."

"I am reminded of the film *Raiders of the Lost Ark*," I told my friend. "Where they hide the Ark of the Covenant inside a crate inside a vast warehouse full of identical crates."

"Just so, Watson, but on an infinitely vaster scale. You see how difficult we have made it for them?"

I had to agree.

"Not only do they have to know about the image in the first place but they then need to locate it within the correct Newsgroup. Then they need to try and crack the password." Holmes laughed. "And the counter-steganography programs are next to useless. There is no way that they can tell if any image contains a secret message or not. There is nothing to give the game away."

"The modern world." I shook my head. "Whatever next?"

"But there is nothing new in steganography, Watson. This is an art that goes back to the dawn of time. Think of invisible ink."

"Oh, yes."

Holmes smiled. "Back in the sixth century BC, Doctor, the tyrant Histiaeus needed to get a message across the front lines to his allies. So he had the head shaved of his most trusted slave and a message tattooed upon the scalp. Once the hair grew back the man was sent on his way and the besieging Persians were stymied. And that, my dear friend, is steganography – from the Greek word *steganos*, meaning 'concealed'."

"Just text documents, Holmes, or can you hide other things?"

"You can hide almost any digital file inside another digital file, only you must be careful not to make the receiving file too large. You could hide one photograph inside another or even video footage in a music file."

"Good heavens."

"Yes, you might even hide top secret plans for an invasion or the blueprints of a nuclear facility within an Adele track on your iPhone."

"I cannot abide that woman. I simply cannot see what all the fuss is about."

Holmes nodded his understanding. "But, Watson, we must now destroy all evidence of An Lee. Seek out the file shredder within Susan's *Platform*."

Whilst I was doing so, I asked my friend a burning question. "But just suppose, Holmes, that my USB thumb drive were to fall into the wrong hands. They would be able to tell that I was an activist straight away. The game would be up."

"There is a simple solution, my friend." Holmes rose from his chair and indicated that I remove my thumb drive. He pointed to it. "Just install the VPN and Tor. Only those. This tells an investigator almost nothing. Now install *Platform* and any other programs directly within a secure cloud store, then access all your tools from there."

"Oh, very clever, Holmes." I stood to follow him out of the room.

"That way, Watson, you only have to memorise the cloud address and your password. Their existence will be your secret. Meanwhile, your adversaries will be busy pouring through your Bulk Data Sets and Internet Connection Record in the belief that they have all the bases covered."

"Well, that has certainly set my mind at rest," I told Holmes as I dashed to catch up. "How about a spot of lunch, Holmes?"

"Yes," he willingly agreed. "Let us sample that new Thai place in Queensway."

CHAPTER ELEVEN
The Dark Arts

"Ah, there you are, Holmes," I declared. "I was wondering what had become of you."

"Have you been waiting long, Doctor?" asked my friend. He tossed his sports bag onto the chaise longue and shuffled out of his wet cape.

"So, you have taken my advice, I see," said I indicating the sports bag. "Have you been exercising down the gym?"

"I have, Watson. Is there tea in that pot or am I too late?"

I got up from my chair before the fire and poured my friend a somewhat stewed cup. "Mrs Hudson let me in and she very kindly made me some tea. There are even a few of my favourite Garibaldi biscuits left."

Holmes plonked himself down and snatched eagerly at a crisp brown wafer. I handed him his cup.

"So, why the sudden change of heart?" I asked. "I have been nagging you for the best part of a year to take exercise."

"I am experiencing a surplus of energy, Doctor. My mind is like a racing engine, tearing itself to pieces. I must burn it off."

"And are you not working on any cases at the moment, Holmes?"

"Not a sausage," huffed my friend. "Romance seems to have passed forever from the criminal world and, as you know, my mind rebels at stagnation."

"Then congratulations, Holmes, for not reverting to your old destructive habits." I was referring, as Holmes knew full well, to his earlier fascination for artificial stimulants – both morphine and cocaine.

"Old hat, old boy," chuckled Holmes. He sipped readily at the dark tea. "You recall my recent foray to Silicon Valley?"

"Consulting work, I believe."

"Yes, my friend. The task itself was nothing to write home about but I did make an interesting discovery whilst there. Have you ever heard of 'micro-dosing', Doctor?"

I let out a deep sigh.

"It is the 'in' thing among the bright young people of the tech world, and most fascinating, too."

"Drugs?" I asked feeling deeply weary.

"In a manner of speaking. Did you ever see that film *Limitless* where a struggling writer somehow acquires a top secret wonder drug that enables him to take full control of his brain? He becomes a financial wizard."

"I did, Holmes. And, as I recall, it did not end well."

My friend shook his head. "This is not quite the same thing but pretty close. Micro-dosing is the act of consuming sub-perceptual amounts of psychedelics, like LSD and *Psilocybin* with the aim of expanding the mind."

"Sub-perceptual meaning the effects are subtle but noticeable?"

"Precisely, Doctor. Typically, individuals integrate sub-perceptual doses into their weekly routine for higher levels of creativity, more energy, increased focus, and improved relationship skills. Micro-dosing also helps to heighten spiritual awareness and enhance all five senses."

I scoffed. "I have never heard of it, Holmes, and I like to pride myself that I keep up-to-date with all the journals. And is it working for you?"

"Indubitably. I take precisely ten micrograms of LSD every four days and it provides the mental exaltation that I crave."

"Where on earth do you get such a thing? You can't just pop down the chemists, can you?"

"I buy it online, Watson. On the Deep Web. Did you bring Susan and your laptop?"

I fished them both out and began to set up. I gave Holmes the nod once I was ready.

***

"I imagine, Doctor, that you were equally surprised to discover the existence of other Internets."

"You could have knocked me over with a feather," I told him.

Holmes smiled. "As you know, it is my business to know what other people don't know. To that end, I have made a particular study of the darker side of the Internet."

"The so-called Dark Net or Dark Web?"

"Just so. Fire up Tor, Watson. We are going to take a walk on the wild side this afternoon. We are going to enter pioneering territory, a place with very few settlers – perhaps half a million daily users as compared to the three billion plus who stay up top."

"Right you are." I had the green screen open in front of me.

"But we must be on our guard, Watson. Many of the natives are hostile. They would like to keep the place to themselves. Others are friendly because they know that more users mean more people to hide among."

"And how big is it, then?"

"Some say this Deep Web is more than five-thousand times the size of the Surface Web – so deep that the major search engines do not venture down there. But, Watson, it is not all dark despite being hidden from view. Just like everything else, there is good and there is bad."

"Where shall we start?"

"Let us go shopping." Holmes sat back and consulted deep within his mind, a far-away look in his eyes. "Our starting point, dear Doctor, is on the Surface Web. VPN first. Then, using Tor, go to deepdotweb.com."

I typed the address into the command line at the top of the page.

"This is a most capital starting point for all things Deep Web, Watson. The good people who run this site stay abreast of all developments and – perhaps just as importantly – they maintain a list of trustworthy vendors and of places where it is safe to do business."

"I am pleased to hear it."

"Follow the links on the home page. Seek out their *Market Comparison Chart*. Here we have a list of the most popular shopping venues. Let us select the one topping the list. Cut and paste the address into a fresh Tor page."

"AlphaBay Market," I announced.

"Sign up. They do not want any personal details. Login and let's see what they have for sale, shall we?" Holmes sprang from his chair and came to look over my shoulder.

"It is much like an eBay or Amazon," I marvelled while scrolling down the home page. "Good heavens, Holmes." I declared. "*Drugs and Chemicals. Counterfeit Items. Credit Cards. Weapons.* How wonderfully shocking." I looked up at Holmes in amazement.

"How much ammunition do you still have for that handgun of yours, Watson?"

"Less than half a box, I shouldn't wonder."

"Then you can restock here, my friend. Click *Weapons*. Click *Ammunition*."

"Blow me down," I declared. I even let out a lengthy whistle. "Lots of 9mm, .38 Special and .45 ACP. They even have ammo for an AK47 or NATO 5.56. I am gob smacked. And very good prices, too."

Holmes smiled. "And they have the guns, Watson. From the security guard's plastic delight – the Glock 17 – through to concealable machine-pistols and long-range sniper rifles. Silencers, too."

"But are they to be trusted? What's to stop them taking your money and then not handing over the goods?"

"Reputation, for one thing. These places work just like eBay. Swindle a buyer and you are booted off the site. Each vendor must lodge a security deposit before they can start listing. It is not worth their while to go around cheating people. This is a market with plenty of willing buyers after all."

"And how do they deliver these guns and the ammo? You can't just pop an SA80 assault rifle in the post – or can you?"

"Seemingly," said Holmes. "They break them down. Ship them off in with machine parts. When all the bits arrive, the buyer looks up on YouTube how to reassemble the thing."

"And this is where one might acquire LSD and other drugs, I imagine." I had returned to the home page.

"When it comes to drugs, Doctor, name your poison. Everything is here."

"And it is all shipped to the buyer in some stealthy manner, I imagine." I shook my head in wonder. "Is there no question of sniffer dogs finding your drugs, Holmes?"

My friend dismissed the notion. "Not a chance. And, besides, most venders will make up any loss if it goes missing. I find it more reliable than any of your usual online shopping haunts."

"Most impressive," I declared. "I applaud any move that takes drugs off the streets."

"Of course, Watson. But that said, we are talking here of the Marketplaces where reputation is everything in a highly competitive arena, where vast fortunes are to be made on commission. Cheats will not be tolerated."

"Yes, I can see that."

"But the same cannot be said of the sole traders that prey – just like their Surface counterparts – upon the unwary and the gullible down here on the Dark Net."

"One can hardly go running to the police," I laughed. "Saying my marijuana or .44 Magnum failed to arrive."

"Precisely. Now, Watson, we are off to the *Hidden Wiki*. Search for it with duckduckgo and paste the address into Tor."

"Here we go," I glanced back at Holmes. "Looks much like Wikipedia."

"For many people, Watson, the *Hidden Wiki* is the gateway to the Onion hidden network. This is a directory of the known unknown, if you will," Holmes nodded sagely.

"There are links to every service imaginable – a distorted mirror image of your Internet – and much of it beyond the realms of the law and much more beyond the realms of common decency."

"Really?"

"You must be alert, Watson. Be careful where you tread. There are people down here who like to lay traps. You might click a link and – suddenly – be confronted by an image so shocking, so utterly depraved and distressing that your mind will be indelibly marked."

"I do not need to remind you, Holmes, that I am a doctor who has seen combat. The most shocking wounds imaginable. I have seen the best of human nature and I have seen the worst."

"You are not so easily shocked," nodded my friend. He straightened back up and took himself off to the window. He was silent for a long time. Finally, he turned and looked me directly in the eyes.

"There are, Watson, truly terrible things to be found here. And I am not even thinking of the people who will commit rape, torture, arson and murder on demand – at your very whim – for a handful of BitCoins."

I shuddered.

"Duels to the death," Holmes grimaced. "Wildlife auctions that would make your heart weep."

"I cannot abide seeing any living creature in distress, Holmes. What sort of auctions?"

"Imagine, Watson, that you are a filthy-rich oligarch. You collect exotic animals. You like to impress your friends and snow leopards are so *passé* these days. What do you get yourself?"

"A panda," I suggested flippantly.

"Precisely, Watson. A panda. But not just any old panda. You want a nice cuddly baby panda. One you can bottle-feed and tuck up in a crib at night."

"Ah, bless."

"But you cannot just pop down the pet shop and have one pulled from a cage for you. You need contacts. The right contacts. There are plenty of pandas in the wild – not just in zoos and shopping malls. And there are people who arrange it all – for a price."

"Dear me."

"And if the vendor should happen to come across a nest of the things, he will auction them off." Holmes held up his hand. "But how do they do that, you ask? I shall tell you, Watson."

Holmes made a move for his violin case and I cringed inwardly. He halted mid-stride and spun back towards me. "First you flick through your contacts book. You seek out the likely buyers. You send them a secret message. You give them an Onion address and a specific window of time."

"I see."

"This Deep Web page will only appear briefly and then it is gone again. You – the buyer Watson – will get a chance to peruse the goods. To see which cuddly little fella takes your fancy. The site goes down. Sometime later you receive another secret message. You go to a different Onion address and there you get your chance to bid. It is quite straightforward."

"Duels to the death, Holmes? What of them?"

"Suppose, Watson. You are the self-same oligarch and you have grown tired of your Filipina chamber maid. And suppose that I am another oligarch and I have much the same thing. Well, we sell them to a Dark Net fight promoter. Same thing as before. You get a secret message, *etcetera*, and you can place your bets while watching the whole grisly thing live."

"Hold on, Holmes. How in the name of all that is good do you ever get two Filipina maids to fight it out to the death? What possible incentive do they have?"

"Elementary, Doctor. You put them both in the picture. The winner gets one-hundred dollars cash and her passport back."

I was shaking my head. "I find this too far fetched, Holmes. I can clearly see the guns and the drugs but these other things – *pandas* – surely not?"

"So right you are, Doctor. Pandas are purely emotive – they are not technically-speaking endangered in that they face imminent extinction. The world's zoos are awash with them."

I felt some relief at that.

"But there are, however, plenty of critically endangered species for auction down here as we speak – creatures like the not-so-cuddly pangolin. You can, of course, buy an adorable baby orang-utan online. And then there are the sad creatures auctioned off for their component parts, like the rhino and tiger and, of course, plenty of elephant ivory."

"And the maids, Holmes?"

"Perhaps not maids fighting to the death, not as such. But an equal level of callousness abounds. Human traffickers buy and sell these women every day. They are treated to the most shocking abuse. Rape and murder are commonplace."

"But live online? Is that really happening?"

My friend scoffed. "Rohinga refugees fleeing Burma are frequently tortured live online by the traffickers – all to get their families to pay up a ransom. The jungles of Thailand are littered with their shallow graves."

I felt sick.

"The Bedouin kidnappers of the Sinai desert, Watson. How do you imagine they best extort money from the distraught friends and families of their victims? The bride market. How else could it function? The enslaved girls filling the brothels of Europe. Where do you imagine that these trades are best carried out?"

"Down here in the depths." I felt choked. "While Lestrade and his ilk spy on us."

"No area of cyberspace a haven," recollected Holmes, stomping to and fro across the living room.

"I could go on, Watson. There are things interminably baser than this. But I do not wish to talk of the lost children who are displayed and abused to the specific directions of those willing to pay and capable of infinite cruelty."

"Please spare me, Holmes."

"We have two distinct but parallel worlds, Doctor. A world where a caring State spends billions to keep us all safe from harm."

"So they tell us."

"And another world where the State shrugs its shoulders when the sick and hopelessly disabled take their own lives because there is no money in the kitty to care for them."

"I know it."

"In this first world, Watson, we blindly hand back to the State the hard-won freedoms of our forebears on the flimsy pretext of protection from future terror. Here we sit quietly by while the State constructs an all-seeing eye – the kind of tool that only a paranoid megalomaniac or totalitarian regime might dream of."

I was shaking my head.

"And in the other world, my friend, we have the criminals, the dealers, the traffickers, the child-abusers – the very people we see here – who are free to operate with impunity. Here the actual terrorists plot, plan and communicate beyond any reach."

"Either Lestrade and his fellows are clueless, Holmes, or they think that we are."

"Let us take an analytical approach, Doctor. The State maintains that it is fighting a war against terror and against organised crime. In order to do so, the State has granted itself unparalleled surveillance powers."

"That is how Lestrade explains it."

"So, Watson, given that we know the terrorists can easily avoid State surveillance, how successful do you suppose the State will be in monitoring the terrorists?"

"Patently, Holmes, it is not possible to catch them by reading people's emails or by spying upon their Internet activities. I must conclude that they will not be successful."

"Precisely," smiled Holmes. "It is not possible. And once we eliminate the impossible, whatever remains – no matter how improbable – must be the truth. You agree?"

"I do. Which means, Holmes, that we are left with the inescapable fact that the State is spying upon us and that – improbably as it may seem – it is not for the stated purpose of keeping us all safe."

"And there you have it, Watson."

"But why, Holmes? Why?"

"Because they see what is coming, my friend. They see the perfect storm."

CHAPTER TWELVE
Storm Coming

Holmes stood and looked out of the window. The lights in the street below glowed amber, adding emphasis to the driving rain as it splattered with force against the glass. I gave the fire a poke and settled back in my chair while my friend continued to gaze outside.

Eventually he cleared his throat and spoke. "I am reminded, Doctor, of the old Chinese curse."

"May you live in interesting times," I put in.

"Yes. That one."

"I should point out, Holmes, that every civilisation in history has thought much the same. The world has always been in chaos and always will be. As the songwriter Billy Joel put it, *We Didn't Start the Fire.*"

"I am inclined to agree with you, Doctor." Holmes turned from the window and began to pace about the snug living room. "That said, there are unique factors at play today. For one, we have never been so reliant upon one single technology – the Internet."

"We might go back to steam and whale oil."

"If there are any whales left," chuffed Holmes as he came to join me beside the fire.

Just then his restless eyes settled upon his infernal vaping machine that sat on the mantelpiece. He soon adjusted the digital settings and was swiftly enveloped in a thick cloud of nauseating elderflower vapour.

"You asked me earlier why the State should wish to spy upon us while leaving the actual criminals and terrorists to their own devices?"

"Yes, I did."

"It is because they know that we are living in truly interesting times. There is an ill wind coming, Watson, and they know it." Holmes expelled another remarkable quantity of vapour. "Information is the only true power."

Dimly I could see that he was holding up his hand and counting on his fingers. I groaned inwardly.

"Economic chaos. Never-ending wars. Countless millions homeless and on the march. Diminishing resources. A shocking divide between rich and poor. Growing disgruntlement and massive unemployment. The rise of nationalism and right-wing politicians…"

Now I had to hold up my hand. "I get the picture, Holmes. And quite frankly most people would rather bury their heads in the sand – and who could blame them?"

"And what of your Internet, Watson, and its glorious ideals? The free flow of thoughts and ideas? The lives immeasurably improved?"

I had to shrug. "Nice idea while it lasted. But what's gone is gone."

"We can reclaim the Internet," declared my friend with vehemence. "Everything you have learnt these past few days will set you free. You can employ the Dark Arts to keep yourself safe, you can employ them for the power of good."

Holmes puffed deeply on his pipe. The room was suddenly so thick with his grey vapour that he was momentarily veiled from sight. Then from deep within the mist my friend spoke in a clear and authoritative voice.

"If they do not know *who* you are. If they do not know *where* you are, they cannot spy upon you, and they cannot fleece you, nor do you harm. Only by opening your eyes to the dangers – and by adopting elementary security measures – do we begin to take back control."

"But seriously," I asked my friend. "Who can be bothered?"

The vaporous clouds began to dissipate.

"Well, fuck it then," said Holmes. "Let's go down the pub."

THE END

About the Authors

Doctor John Watson is the celebrated chronicler of Sherlock Holmes, the world's greatest detective. He received his medical degree from Barts and the University of London before training as an assistant surgeon in the British Army. He was wounded while serving in Afghanistan.

In the writing of this book, Dr Watson has called upon the services of **Alan Pearce**, a renowned cyber-security expert and author of numerous books who lectures around the world and trains journalists and others in digital counter-surveillance. He was also wounded in Afghanistan – while serving as the BBC Kabul Correspondent.

Useful Links

Avast - https://www.avast.com
Hotspot Shield - https://www.hotspotshield.com
Signal - https://whispersystems.org/
Smartphone Spy Apps -
http://www.hongkiat.com/blog/iphone-spy-apps/
Ear Spy - http://www.overpass.co.uk/app/ear-spy/
Ship Finder - http://shipfinder.co/about/
Tresorit - https://tresorit.com/
Seafile Secure Cloud Storage -
https://www.seafile.com/en/home/
FinSpy - https://wikileaks.org/spyfiles/files/0/289_GAMMA-
201110-FinSpy.pdf
Fake Tweets - http://www.lemmetweetthatforyou.com/
Expand Short Links - http://checkshorturl.com/
No More Ransom - https://www.nomoreransom.org/
Angry IP Scanner - http://angryip.org/
Shodan - https://www.shodan.io/
Philips HUE lighting system - http://www2.meethue.com
Mozilla Firefox - https://www.mozilla.org/en-US/firefox/new/
Firefox Add-Ons - https://addons.mozilla.org/en-US/firefox/
Open Office Suite - https://www.openoffice.org/
VLC media player - http://www.videolan.org/vlc/index.html
Foxit PDF Reader -
https://www.foxitsoftware.com/products/pdf-reader/
Recommended VPNs – https://www.deepdotweb.com/vpn-
comparison-chart/
Tor Onion Browser - https://www.torproject.org/
Evidence Nuker - http://www.evidencenuker.com/
AnonyMouse Email Remailer -
http://anonymouse.org/anonemail.html
Unseen Email - https://unseen.is/
PrivNote - https://privnote.com/#
PGP Pretty Good Privacy - http://www.pgpi.org/

Platform Operating System - http://portableapps.com/download
Recommended Search Engines - https://duckduckgo.com/ and see http://www.howtogeek.com/113513/5-alternative-search-engines-that-respect-your-privacy/
Newsbin - http://www.newsbin.com/
Usenet - http://www.usenet.com/
OpenStego - http://www.openstego.com/
Deepdotweb - https://www.deepdotweb.com/
Hidden Wiki - https://thehiddenwiki.org/

Also recommended:
http://www.wonderhowto.com/

Recommended Reading

DEEP WEB SECRECY & SECURITY
By Conrad Jaeger & Alan Pearce

A 'MUST READ' guide to protecting yourself against Big Brother for novice and expert alike, says the hacktivist group Anonymous. Use the secrets of the Deep Web to protect you and your family, your private and business interests, your views and your freedoms.

DEEP WEB FOR JOURNALISTS: Comms, Counter-Surveillance, Search
By Alan Pearce

Being a journalist in 2017 is more dangerous than it ever was. We are now being actively targeted online by intelligence agencies, law enforcement and others. "Offers an uncompromising diagnosis of the perils of online communications and should shatter the confidence many of us place in the unguarded ways of working online," says Jim Boumelha, President of International Federation of Journalists.

MAKE YOUR SMARTPHONE 007 SMART
By Conrad Jaeger & Alan Pearce

The smartphone in your pocket can easily be turned into a high-tech spy tool and counter-surveillance device to rival anything that Ian Fleming's Q might have dreamt up. "An amazing eye-opener!"

DEEP SEARCH: How to Search the Internet More Effectively
By Alan Pearce

Find what you're looking for in a fraction of the time. This enlightening and easy interactive e-book will improve your search skills; cutting the time you spend trawling the Web for whatever you want. The perfect tool for anyone who seriously needs to search the Internet – journalists, students, researchers, law enforcement and librarians.

Contact

ALAN PEARCE by email: holmes@alanpearce.com

Printed in Great Britain
by Amazon